Andrew Carnegie

Our coaching Trip

Brighton to Inverness

Andrew Carnegie

Our coaching Trip
Brighton to Inverness

ISBN/EAN: 9783337146269

Printed in Europe, USA, Canada, Australia, Japan

Cover: Foto ©Andreas Hilbeck / pixelio.de

More available books at **www.hansebooks.com**

OUR

COACHING TRIP

BRIGHTON TO INVERNESS

BY
ANDREW CARNEGIE.

(PRIVATE CIRCULATION.)

NEW YORK.
1882.

"Ah, that such beauty cannot be portrayed
 By words, nor by the pencil's silent skill,
 But is the property of him alone
 Who hath beheld it, noted it with care,
 And in his mind recorded it with love."

TO MY BROTHER

AND TRUSTY ASSOCIATES,

WHO TOILED AT HOME THAT I MIGHT REALIZE THE HAPPIEST

DREAM OF MY LIFE, THIS RECORD, LIKE "ROUND THE

WORLD," IS ALSO AFFECTIONATELY

INSCRIBED BY THE

GRATEFUL AUTHOR.

NEW YORK, *March* 10, 1882.

OUR COACHING TRIP.

Bang! click! once more the desk closes and the key turns! Not "Round the World" again, but "Ho for England, for England!" is the cry, and "Scotland's hills and Scotland's dales and Scotland's vales for me."

Long enough ago to permit us to sing,

"For we are boys, merry, merry boys,"

and the world lay all before us where to choose, Dod, Vandy, Harry, and I walked through Southern England with knapsacks on our backs. What pranks we played! Those were the happy days when we heard the chimes at midnight and laughed Sir Prudence out of countenance. "Dost thou think, because thou art virtuous, there shall be no more cakes and ale?" Nay, verily, Sir Gray Beard, and ginger shall be hot i' the mouth too! Then indeed

"The sounding cataract
Haunted me like a passion; the tall rock,
The mountain, and the deep and gloomy wood,
Their colors and their forms, were then to me
An appetite: a feeling and a love
That had no need of a remoter charm,
By thought supplied, or any interest
Unborrowed from the eye."

It was during this pedestrian excursion that I announced that some day, when my "ships came home," I should drive a party of my dearest friends from Brighton to Inverness. Black's "Adventures of a Phaeton" came not long after this to prove that another Scot had divined how idyllic the journey could be made. It was something of an air-castle—of a dream--those far-off days, but see how it has come to pass!

The world, in my opinion, is all wrong on the subject of air-castles. People are forever complaining that their châteaux en Espagne are never realized. But the trouble is with them—they fail to recognize them when they come. "To-day," says Carlyle, "is a king in disguise," and most people are in possession of their air-castles, but lack the trick to see't.

Look around you! see Vandy, for instance. When we were thus doing Merrie England on foot, he with a very modest letter of credit stowed away in a belt round his sacred person—for Vandy it was who always carried the bag (and a faithful treasurer and a careful one too—good boy, Vandy!); he was a poor student then, and you should have heard him philosophize and lord it over us two, who had been somewhat fortunate in rolling mills and were devoted to business. "Great Cæsar! boys, if I ever get fifteen hundred dollars a year income!" (This was the fortune I was vaguely figured up to be worth under ordinary conditions.) "Great Cæsar! boys" —and here the fist would come down on the hard deal table, spilling a few drops of beer—"fifteen hundred dollars a year! Catch me working any more like a slave, as you and Harry do!" Well, well, Vandy's air-castle was fifteen hundred dollars a year, yet see him now when thousands roll in upon him every month. Hard at it still—and see the goddess laughing in her sleeve at the good joke on Vandy. He has his air-castle, but doesn't recognize the structure.

There is Miss Fashion. How fascinating she was when she descanted on her air-castle—then a pretty cottage with white and red roses clustering beside the door and twining over it in a true-lovers' knot, symbolizing the lover's ideal of mutual help and dependence—the white upon the red. No large establishment for her, nor many servants! One horse (I admit it was always to be a big one), and an elegant little vehicle; plenty of garden and enough of pin-money. On this point there was never to be the slightest doubt, so that she could really get the best magazines and one new book every month—any one she chose. A young hard-working husband, without too much income, so that she might experience the pleasure of planning to make their little go far. Behold her now! her husband a millionaire, a brown-stone front, half a dozen horses, a country place, and a box at the opera! But, bless your heart! she is as unconscious of the arrival of her castle as she is that years creep upon her apace.

The Goddess Fortune, my friends, rarely fails to give to mortals all they pray for and more, but how she must stand amazed at the blindness of her idolaters who continue to offer up their prayers at her shrine wholly unconscious that their first requests have been granted. It takes Fortune a little time to prepare the gifts for so many supplicants—the toys each one specially wants; and lo and behold! before they can be delivered (though she works with speed betimes) the unreasonable mortals have lost conceit of their prizes, and their coming is a mockery; they are crying for something else. If the Fates be malignant, as old religions teach, how they must enjoy the folly of man!

Imagine a good spirit taking Fortune to task for the misery and discontent of mortals, as she gazes with piteous eyes upon our disappointments, our troubles, and, saddest of all, our regrets, charging her with producing such unhappiness. "Why have you done this?" would be the inquiry. Listen to the sardonic chuckle of the Fate: "Hush! I've only given them what they asked (chuckle—chuckle—chuckle)! Not my fault! See that unhappy wretch, sleeplessly and feverishly tossing on his pillow, and in his waking hours absorbing all his lofty faculties in gambling at the Stock Exchange—wife, children, home, music, art, culture, all forgotten. He was once a bright, promising, ingenuous youth. He was born among trees and green fields, spent the morn of life in the country, sensitive and responsive to all nature's whisperings; lay in cool, leafy shades, wandered in forest glades, and paddled in the 'complaining brooks which make the meadow green.' Nay, not many years ago he returned at intervals to these scenes and found their charm had still power over him—felt the truth of the poet's words, that

"' To him who in the love of nature holds
Communion with her visible forms, she speaks

> A various language ; for his gayer hours
> She has a voice of gladness, and a smile
> And eloquence of beauty, and she glides
> Into his darker musings, with a mild
> And healing sympathy, that steals away
> Their sharpness, ere he is aware.'

"He asked for enough to live honorably upon among his fellows," continues the Fate, "and to keep his parents comfortable in their old age—a matter of a few hundreds a year—and I gave him this and thousands more. Ha, ha, ha! silence! Look at him; he doesn't see the joke. You may try to tell it to him, if you like. He has no time to listen, nor ears to hear, nor eyes to see ; no, nor soul to understand your language. He's 'short' on New Jersey Central or 'long' on Reading, and, bless you! he must strain every fibre if he would save himself from ruin.

"He could commune with you in your youth, you say; he had your language then. No doubt! no doubt! so did he then know his Latin and whisper his prayers at his mother's knee. The Latin has gone ; his praying continues - nay has increased, for his fears and selfish wants have multiplied since he was an innocent, ignorant child, and he has much more to ask from God for his own ends, now that he is a wise man and is supposed to know much (chuckle—chuckle—chuckle).

"There is another mortal," we hear the Fate saying to the Good Fairy. "Look at her, decked out in all the vagaries of changeable Fashion ; note her fixed-up look, her conventional air, her nervous, unmeaning, simpering smile—the same to-day, yesterday, and forever—something to all men, much to none. See her at home in her chamber! Why mopes she, looking so haggard, with features expressionless and inane? What worm gnaws at her heart and makes her life so petty? She too came into the world a bright and happy thing, and grew up fond of music and of birds, and with a passion for flowers and all of Nature's sweets; so careful too of mother and of father, the very embodiment of love to all around her. You should have seen her in her teens, a glorious ray from heaven—'making a sunshine in a shady place'—so natural, so hearty, with a carolling laugh like the falling of waters. In her most secret prayers she asked only for a kind lover with a fair competence, that they might live modestly, without ostentation. She was a good girl and I gave her her wish and more," says Fate. "Her air-castle was small, but I sent her a magnificent one. She is courted, flattered, has every gift in my power to bestow; yet she pines in the midst of them. The fruits of her rare gardens have no flavor for her—Dead Sea fruits indeed, which fall to ashes on her lips. She has entered for the race of Fashion, and her soul is absorbed in its jealousies and disappointments. You may speak to her as of old; tell her there is something noble in that domain of human life where duties grow—something not only beyond but different from Fashion, higher than dress or show. She understands you not.

"Hand her a bunch of violets. Does she learn their lesson with their odor (which her dog scents as well as she)? Comes there to her the inner meaning, the scent of the new-mown hay that speaks of past hours of purity, of the fresh breeze that fanned her cheek in childhood's halcyon days, the love of all things of the green earth and the sense of the goodness of God which his flowers ever hold within their petals for those who know their language? 'They will decorate me to-night for the ball!' That is the be-all and the end-all of her ladyship's love for flowers.

"Show her a picture with more of heaven than earth in it, and glimpses of the light that never shone on sea or shore. If the artist be in fashion she will call it 'pretty' when it is grand. Give her music. Is it the opera? Oh, yes, she will attend. It is the fashion. But place within her reach the soul-moving oratorio (with more religion in it than in twenty sermons) or the suggestive symphony. No, a previous engagement prevents. Why, just think of it —*one can't talk there!* Yet this woman could once play with feeling and sing with expression, delighting her young companions. Of her one could truly say,

"'Oh! to see or hear her singing! scarce I know which is divinest—
For her looks sing too—she modulates her gestures on the tune;
And her mouth stirs with the song, like song; and when the notes are finest,
'Tis the eyes that shoot out vocal light, and seem to swell them on.'

And now she has fallen to this!"

"Has she children?" inquires the Good Spirit. "Oh," says Fate, "we are not altogether relentless. How could we give such a woman children and look you in the face? It is sometimes thought necessary even to go as far as this, but in such cases we commend the poor infants to the special care of the great

Father, for mother they have none. But look! there is a man now who did so pray for a son and heir that we gave him one, and yonder goes the result. God in heaven! why are men so rash in their blindness as to pray for anything! Surely 'Thy will be done' were best."

I am as bad as Sterne in his "Sentimental Journey," and will never get on at this rate. I started to argue that the Fates were too kind instead of not kind enough; at least, my air-castles have ever been mere toys compared with the realities, for never did I dream, in my wildest days, that the intended drive through Britain would assume the princely proportions of a four-in-hand, crowded with a dozen of my dearest friends. A modest phaeton or wagonette with a pair of horses was the extent of my dream, but the Fairy sent me four, you see, and two friends for every one I had pleased myself with imagining as sure to take the journey with me.

But now to a sober beginning of the story of the coach. It was in the leafy month of June—the very first day thereof, however—in the year of our Lord 1881, that the good ship Bothnia (Cunard Line, of course), Captain McMicken (a true Scot and bold British sailor), steamed from the future Metropolis of the World for the shores of Merrie England. She had many passengers, but among them were eleven who outranked all others, if their respective opinions of each other were to be accepted as the true standard of judgment. I had received for several months before the sweetest pleasure imaginable in startling first one and then another with requests to report at headquarters, Windsor Hotel, New York, May 31st, prepared to embark. It was on St. Valentine's Day that Miss Jeannie Johns received a missive which caused her young heart to flutter. What a pretty reply came! Here is a short extract:

"Three months to dream of it; three months to live in it; and my whole lifetime afterward to think it over. I am the happiest girl alive, only sometimes I can't believe it's all going to happen."

To Davenport, Iowa, went another invitation. In due time came a return missive from the proud City of the River:

"Will I go to Paradise for three months on a coach? Agent of Providence, I will!"

Isn't it glorious to make one's friends so happy?

HARBOR OF NEW YORK, June 1, 1881.
On board Steamer Bothnia.

Call the roll.

Lady Dowager Mother, Head of the Clan (no Salic Law in our family); Miss Jeannie Johns (Prima Donna); Miss Alice French (Stewardess); Mr. and Mrs. McCargo (Dainty Davie); Mr. and Mrs. King (Paisley Troubadours, Aleck good for fun and Aggie good for everything); Benjamin F. Vandevort (Benjie); Henry Phipps, Jr. (H. P., Our Pard); G. F. McCandless (General Manager); ten in all, making together with the scribe the All-coaching Eleven.

Ting-a-ling-a-ling! The tears are shed, the kisses ta'en. The helpless hulk breathes the breath of life. The pulsations of its mighty heart are felt; the last rope that binds us to land cast off, and now see the hundreds of handkerchiefs waving from the pier fading and fading away. But note among the wavers one slight graceful figure: Miss Mary Clark of our party, present in spirit if bodily absent on duty, much to the regret of us all. The wavings from deck to shore tell our friends

> "how slow our souls sailed on,
> How fast our ship."

The Bothnia turned her face to the east, and out upon old ocean's gray and melancholy waste sailed the Gay Charioteers. As we steamed down the bay three steamers crowded with the most enterprising of Europe's people passed us, emigrants coming to find in the bounteous bosom of the Great Republic the blessings of equality, the just reward of honest labor. Ah, favored land! the best of the Old World seek your shores to swell to still grander proportions your assured greatness. That all come only for the material benefits you confer, I do not believe. Crowning these material considerations, I insist that the more intelligent of these people feel the spirit of true manhood stirring within them, and glory in the thought that they are to become part of a powerful people, of a government founded upon the born equality of man, free from military despotism and class distinctions. There is a trace of the serf in the man who lives contentedly in a land with ranks above him. One hundred and seventeen thousand came last month, and the cry is still they come! O ye self-constituted rulers of men in Europe, know you not that the knell of dynasties and of rank is sounding? Are you so deaf that you do not hear the thunders, so blind that you do not see the lightnings which now and then give warning of the storm that is to precede the reign of the people?

There is everything in the way one takes things. "Whatever is, is right," is a good maxim for travellers to adopt, but the Charioteers improved on that. The first resolution they passed was, "Whatever is, is lovely; all that does happen and all that doesn't shall be altogether lovely." We shall quarrel with nothing, admire everything and everybody. A surly beggar shall afford us sport, if any one can be surly under our smiles; and stale bread and poor fare shall only serve to remind us that we have banqueted at the Windsor. Even no dinner at all shall pass for a good joke. Rain shall be hailed as good for the growing corn; a cold day pass as invigorating, a warm one welcomed as suggestive of summer at home, and even a Scotch mist serve to remind us of the mysterious ways of Providence. In this mood the start was made. Could any one suggest a better for our purpose?

Now comes a splendid place to skip—the ocean voyage. Everybody writes that up upon the first trip, and every family knows all about it from the long descriptive letters of the absent one doing Europe.

When one has crossed the Atlantic twenty odd times there seems just about as much sense in boring one's readers with an account of the trip as if the journey were by rail from New York to Chicago. We had a fine, smooth run, and though some of us were a trifle distrait, most of us were supremely happy. A sea voyage compared with land travel is a good deal like matrimony compared with single blessedness, I take it : either decidedly better or decidedly worse. To him who finds himself comfortable at sea, the ocean is the grandest of treats. He never fails to feel himself a boy again while on the waves. There is an exaltation about it. " He walks the monarch of the peopled deck," glories in the storm, rises with and revels in it. Heroic song comes to him. The ship becomes a live thing, and if the monster rears and plunges it is akin to bounding on his thoroughbred who knows its rider. Many men feel thus, and I am happily of them, but the ladies who are at their best at sea are few.

The travellers, however, bore the journey well, though one or two proved indifferent sailors. One morning I had to make several calls upon members below and administer my favorite remedy ; but pale and dejected as the patients were, not one failed to smile a ghastly smile, and repeat after a fashion the cabalistic words—" Altogether lovely."

In no branch of human progress has greater advance been made within the past twenty years than in ocean navigation by steam ; not so much in the matter of speed as in cost of transport. The Persia, once the crack ship of the Cunard Line, required an expenditure of thirty-five dollars as against her successors' one dollar. The Servia will carry thirty-five tons across the ocean for what one ton cost in the Persia. A revolution indeed ! and one which brings the products of American soil close to the British shores.

Quite recently flour has been carried from Chicago to Liverpool for about eighty cents per barrel. The farmer of Illinois is as near the principal markets of Britain as the farmer in England who grows his crops one hundred miles from his market and transports by rail.

Some of the good people of Britain who are interested in land believe that the competition of America has reached its height. Deluded souls, it has only begun!

One cannot be a day at sea without meeting the American who regrets that the Stars and Stripes has been commercially driven from the ocean. This always reminds me of a fable of the lion and the turtle. The lion was proudly walking along the shore, the real king of his domain, the land. The turtle mocked him, saying, Oh, that's nothing, any one can walk on land. Let's see you try it in the water. The lion tried. Result: the turtle fed upon him for many days. America can only render herself ridiculous by entering the water. That is, England's domain.

"Her home is on the mountain wave,
Her march is o'er the deep."

Travellers know the character and abilities of the men in charge of a Cunard ship, but have they ever considered for what pittances such men are obtained? Captain, $3250 per annum; first officer, $1000; second, third, and fourth officers, $600. For what sum think you can be had a man capable of controlling the ponderous machinery of the Servia? Chief engineer, $1250. You have seen the firemen at work down below, perhaps. Do you know any work so hard as this? Price $30 per month. The first cost of a steel ship—and it is scarcely worth while in these days to think of any other kind—is about one half on the Clyde what it is on the Delaware. Steel can be made, and is made, in Britain for one half its cost here. Not in our day will it be wise for America to leave the land. It is a very fair division, as matters stand—the land for America, the sea for England.

FRIDAY, June 10, 1881.

Land ahoy! There it was, the long dark low-lying cloud which was no cloud, but the outline of one of the most unfortunate of lands—unhappy Ireland, cursed by the well-meaning attempt of England to grow Englishmen there. England's experience north of the Tweed should have taught her better.

We reached Liverpool Saturday morning. How pleasant it is to step on shore in a strange land and be greeted by kind friends on the quay! Their welcome to England counted for so much.

Mr. and Mrs. Pullman had been fellow-passengers. A special car was waiting to take them to London, but they decided not to go, and Mr. Pullman very kindly placed it at the disposal of Mr. Jones and family (who were, fortunately for us, also fellow-passengers) and our party, so that we began our travelling upon the other side under unexpectedly favorable conditions.

To such of the party as were getting their first glimpse of the beautiful isle, the journey to London seemed an awakening from happy dreams. They had dreamt England looked thus and thus, and now their dreams had come true. The scenery of the Midland route is very fine, much more attractive than that of the other line.

The party spent from Saturday until Thursday at the Westminster Hotel, in monster London, every one being free to do what most interested him or her. Groups of three or four were formed for this purpose by the law of natural selection, but the roll was called for breakfasts and dinners, so that we all met daily and were fully advised of each other's movements.

The House of Commons claimed the first place with our party, all being anxious to see the Mother of Parliaments. It is not so easy a matter to do this as to see our Congress in session ; but thanks to our friend Mr. Robert Clark and to others, we were fortunate in being able to do so frequently. Our ladies had the pleasure of being taken into the Ladies' Gallery by one of the rising statesmen of England, Sir Charles Dilke, a Cabinet Minister, and one who has had the boldness, and as I think the rare sagacity, to say that he prefers the republican to the monarchical system of government. The world is to hear of Sir Charles Dilke if he live and health be granted him.

We really heard John Bright speak—the one of all men living whom our party wished most to see and to hear. I had not forgotten hearing him speak in Dunfermline, when I was seven years of age, and well do I remember that when I got home I told mother he made one mistake ; for when speaking of Mr. Smith (the Liberal candidate), he called him a *men*, instead of a *maan*. When introduced to Mr. Bright I was delighted to find that he had not forgotten Dunfermline, nor Erskine Beveridge, nor Uncle Morrison.

A grand character, that of the sturdy Quaker; once the best hated man in Britain, but one to whom both continents are now glad to confess their gratitude. He has been wiser than his generation, but has lived to see it grow up to him. Certainly no American can look down from the gallery upon that white head without beseeching heaven to shower its choicest blessings upon it. He spoke calmly upon the Permissive Liquor Bill, and gave the ministerial statement in regard to it. All he said was good common sense; we could do something by regulating the traffic and confining it to reasonable hours, but after all the great cure must come from the better education of the masses, who must be brought to feel that it is unworthy of their manhood to brutalize themselves with liquor. England has set herself at last to the most important of all work—the thorough education of her people; and we may confidently expect to see a great improvement in their habits in the next generation. My plan for mastering the monster evil of intemperance is that our temperance societies, instead of pledging men never to taste alcoholic beverages, should be really temperance agencies and require their members to use them only at meals—never to drink wines or spirits without eating. The man who takes a glass of wine, or beer, or spirits at dinner is clearly none the worse for it. I judge that if the medical fraternity were polled, a large majority would say he was the better for it. Why can't we recognize the fact that all races indulge in stimulants and will continue to do so? It is the regulation, not the eradication, of this appetite that is practical. The coming man is to consider it low to walk up to a bar and gulp down liquor. The race will come to this platform generations before they will accept that of Sir Wilfred Lawson and his total abstinence ideas.

Mr. Conway's article in *Harper's* upon Bedford Square, which gave glowing accounts of this Arcadian colony, with its æsthetic homes, its Tabard Inn, and its club, gave us all a great desire to visit it. We did so one afternoon, and received a very cordial welcome from Mrs. Conway in the absence of her husband. She kindly showed us the grounds and explained all to us. Truth compels me to say we were sadly disappointed, but for this we had probably only ourselves to blame. It is so natural to imagine that exquisite wood-cuts and pretty illustrations set forth grander things than they do. The houses were much inferior to our preconceived ideas, and many had soft woods painted, and most of the cheap shams of ordinary structures. The absence of grand trees, shady dells, and ornamental grounds, and the exceedingly cheap and cheap-looking houses made all seem like a new settlement in the Far West rather than the latest development of culture.

From this criticism Mr. Conway's own pretty little home is wholly exempt, and no doubt there are many other homes there equally admirable. I speak only of the general impression made upon our party, who were all decidedly of opinion that the most charming object there was Mrs. Conway herself.

Extremes meet. It was from houses such as I have spoken of that we went direct to Stafford House, to meet the Marquis of Stafford by appointment, and to be shown over that palace by him. What a change! If the former were not up to our expectations, this exceeded them. I don't suppose any one ever has expected to see such a staircase as enchants him upon entering Stafford House. This is the most magnificent residence any of us has ever seen. I will not trust myself to speak of its beauties, nor of the treasures it contains. One begins to understand to what the Marquis of Stafford is born. The Sutherland family has a million two hundred thousand acres of land in Britain; no other family in the world compares with it as a landowner. It is positively startling to think of it. Almost the entire County of Sutherland is theirs. Stafford House is their London residence. They have Trentham Hall and Lillieshall in Mid England, and glorious Dunrobin Castle in Scotland.

The Marquis sits in the House of Commons as member for Sutherland County, and what do you think! he is a painstaking director of the London and North-Western Railway, and I am informed pays strict attention to its affairs. The Duke of Devonshire is Chairman of the Barrow Steel Company. Lord Granville has iron works, and Earl Dudley is one of the principal iron manufacturers of England. It is all right, you see, my friends, to be a steel-rail manufacturer or an iron-master. How fortunate! But the line must be drawn somewhere, and we draw it at trade. The A. T. Stewarts and the Morrisons have no standing in society in England. They are in vulgar trade. Now if they brewed beer, for instance, they would be somebodies.

We heard a performance of the "Messiah" in Albert Hall, which Miss Johns agreed with me was better in two important particulars than any similar performance we had heard in America. First in vigor of attack by the chorus; this was superb, from the first instant the full volume and quality of sound were perfect. The other point was that all-important one of pronunciation. We have no chorus in New York which rivals what we heard. The words were of course familiar, and we could scarcely judge whether we were correct in our impression, but we believed that even had they been strange to us we could nevertheless have understood every word. Since my return to New York I have heard this oratorio given by the Oratorio Society, and am delighted to note that Dr. Damrosch has greatly improved his chorus in this respect, but the English do pronounce perfectly in singing. This opinion was confirmed by the music subsequently heard in various places throughout our travels. In public as well as in private singing the purity of pronunciation struck us as remarkable. If I ever set up for a music teacher I shall bequeath to my favorite pupil as the secret of success but one word, "*pronunciation.*"

Some of us went almost every day to Westminster, but dancing attendance upon Parliament is much like doing so upon Congress. The interesting debates are few and far between. The daily routine is uninteresting, and one sees how rapidly all houses of legislation are losing their hold upon public attention. A debate upon the propriety of allowing Manchester to dispose of her sewage to please herself, or of permitting Dunfermline to bring in a supply of water, seems such a waste of time. The Imperial Parliament of Great Britain seems much in want of something to do when it condescends to occupy its time with trifling questions which the community interested can best settle; but even in matters of national importance debates are no longer what they were. The questions have already been threshed out in the Reviews—those coming forums of discussion—and all that can be said already said by writers upon both sides of the question who know its bearings much better than the leaders of party. When the *Fortnightly* or the *Nineteenth Century* gets through with a subject, the Prime Minister only rises to sum up the result at which the Morleys and Rogerses and Huxleys have previously arrived.

The English are prone to contrast the men of America and England who are in political life, and the balance is no doubt greatly in their favor. But the reason lies upon the surface: America has solved the fundamental questions of government, and no changes are desired of sufficient moment to engage the minds of her ablest men. During the civil war, when new issues arose and had to be met, the men who stepped forward to guide the nation were of an entirely different class from those prominent in politics either before or since. Contrast the men of Buchanan's administration with those the war called to the front—Lincoln, Seward, Stanton, Sumner, Edmunds, Morton, or the generals with Grant,

Sherman, Sheridan, Hancock. All of these men I
have known well, except one or two of the least prominent.
I have met some of the best known politicians
in England. Compared morally or intellectually,
I do not think there is much, if any, difference
between them; while for original creative power I
believe the Americans superior. That a band of men
so remarkable as to cause surprise to other nations
will promptly arise whenever there is real work to
do, no one who knows the American people can
doubt; but no man of real ability is going to spend
his energies endeavoring to control appointments to
the New York Custom House, any more than he
will continue very long to waste his time discussing
Manchester sewage. Much as my English friends
dislike to believe it, I tell them that when there is
really no great work to be done, when the conflict
between feudal and democratic ideas ends, as it is
fast coming to an end, and there is no vestige of
privilege left from throne to knighthood, only vain,
weak men will seek election to Parliament, and such
will stand ready to do the bidding of the constituencies
as our agents in Congress do. But this need
not alarm our English friends; there will then be
much less bribery before election and much less succumbing
to social court influences after it. The
brains of a country will be found where the real
work is to do. The House of Lords registers
the decrees of the House of Commons. The House
of Commons is soon to register the decrees of the
monthlies. Both these things may be pronounced
good. In the next generation the debates of Parliament
will affect the political currents of the age

as little as the fulminations of the pulpit affect religious thought at present; and then a man who feels he has real power within him will think of entering Parliament about as soon as he would think of entering the House of Lords or the American Congress.

"The parliament of man, the federation of the world,"

comes on apace; but its form is to be largely impersonal. The press is the universal parliament. The leaders in that forum make your "statesman" dance as they pipe.

The same law is robbing the pulpit of real power. Who cares what the Reverend Mr. Froth preaches nowadays, when he ventures beyond the homilies? Three pages by Professor Robertson Smith in the "Encyclopædia Britannica" destroy more theology in an hour than all the preachers in the land can build up in a lifetime. If any man wants *bona fide* substantial power and influence in this world, he must handle the pen—that's flat. Truly, it is a nobler weapon than the sword, and a much nobler one than the tongue, both of which have nearly had their day.

We had a happy luncheon with our good friends the Clarks, one of our London days, and some of our party who had heard that there was not a great variety of edibles in England saw reason to revise their ideas. Another day we had a notable procession for miles through London streets and suburbs to the residence of our friend, Mr. Beck. Five hansoms in line driven pell-mell reminded me of our Tokio experiences with Ginrikshaws, two Bettos tandem in each.

It was a pretty, graceful courtesy, my friend, to display from the upper window the "Stars and Stripes," in honor of the arrival of your American guests, and prettier still to have across your hall as a portière, under which all must bow as they entered, that flag which tells of a government founded upon the born equality of man. Thanks! Such things touch the heart as well as the patriotic chord which vibrates in the breast of every one so fortunate as to claim that glorious standard as the emblem of the land he fondly calls his own. Colonel Robert Ingersoll, that wonderful orator, says that when abroad, after a long interval, he saw in one of the seaports the Stars and Stripes fluttering in the breeze, "he felt the air had blossomed into joy." It was he too who told the South long ago that "there wasn't air enough upon the American continent to float two flags." Right there, Colonel!

Do you know why the American worships his flag with an intenser passion than even the Briton does? I will tell you. It is because it is not the flag of a government which discriminates between her children, decreeing privilege to one and denying it to another, but the flag of the people which gives the same rights to all. The British flag was born too soon to be close to the masses. It came before their time, when they had little or no power. They were not consulted about it. Some conclave made it as a Pope is made and handed it down to the nation. But the American flag bears in every fibre the warrant, "We the People in Congress assembled." It is their own child, and how supremely it is beloved!

It is a significant fact that in no riot or local

outbreak have soldiers of the United States, bearing the national flag, ever been assaulted. Militia troops have sometimes been stoned, but United States troops never. During the worst riot ever known in America, that in our own good city of Pittsburgh, Pennsylvania, twenty-eight United States soldiers, all there were in the barracks, marched through the thousands of excited men unmolested. I really believe that had any man in the crowd dared to touch that flag, General Dix's famous order would have been promptly enforced by his companions. I recently asked Major-General Hancock whether he had ever known United States soldiers to be attacked by citizens, and he said he never had. He was in command of the troops during the riots in the coal regions in Pennsylvania some years ago, and whenever a body of his regulars appeared they were respected and peace reigned.

General Dix's order was, "If any man touches the Stars and Stripes shoot him on the spot." So say we all of us. And it will be the same in Britain some day, ay and in Ireland too, when an end has been made of privilege and there is not a government and a people, but only a government of the people, for the people, and by the people. That day is not so far off either as some of you think, mark me.

But good-bye, London, and all the thoughts which crowd upon one when in your mighty whirl. You monster London, we are all glad to escape you! But ere we "gang awa'" shall we not note our visit to one we are proud to call our friend, and of whom Scotland is proud, Dr. Samuel Smiles, a writer of books indeed—books which influence his own generation much, and the younger generation more. Burns's wish was that he

> "For poor auld Scotland's sake
> Some useful plan or book could make,
> Or sing a sang at least."

Well, the Doctor has made several books that are books, and I have heard him sing a song, too, for the days of Auld Lang Syne. May he live long, and long may his devoted wife be spared to watch over him!

THURSDAY MORNING, June 16, 1881.

We are off for Brighton. Mr. and Miss Beck accompany us. Mr. and Mrs. King have run up to Paisley with the children to get them settled with the doting grandparents, and Mr. and Mrs. Graham have joined us in their place. The coach, horses, and servants went down during the night.

We had time to visit the unequalled aquarium and to do the parade before dinner. Miss French and I stole off to make a much more interesting visit; we called upon William Black, whose acquaintance I had been fortunate enough to make in Rome, and whom I had told that I should some day imitate his "Adventures of a Phaeton." A week before we sailed from New York I had dined with President Garfield at Secretary Blaine's in Washington. After dinner, conversation turned upon my proposed journey, and the President became much interested. "It is the 'Adventures of a Phaeton' on a grand scale," he remarked. "By the way, has Black ever written any other story quite so good as that? I do not think he has." In this there was a general concurrence. He then said: "But I am provoked with Black just now. A man who writes to entertain has no right to end a story as miserably as he has done that of 'MacLeod of Dare.' Fiction should give us the bright side of existence. *Real life has tragedies enough of its own.*"

A few weeks more and we were to have in his own case the most terrible proof of the words he had spoken so solemnly. I can never forget the sad, careworn expression of his face as he uttered them.

> "But come it soon or come it fast,
> It is but death that comes at last."

One might almost be willing to die if, as in Garfield's case, there should flash from his grave, at the touch of a mutual sorrow, to both divisions of the great English-speaking race, the knowledge that they are brothers. This discovery will bear good fruit in time.

> "Nothing in his life became him like the leaving it."

Garfield's life was not in vain. It tells its own story—this poor boy toiling upward to the proudest position on earth, the elected of fifty millions of freemen, a position compared with which that of king or kaiser is as nothing. Let other nations ask themselves where are *our* Lincolns and Garfields? Ah, they grow not except where all men are born equal! The cold shade of aristocracy nips them in the bud.

Mr. Black came to see us off, but arrived at our starting-place a few minutes too late. A thousand pities! Had we only known that he intended to do us this honor, until high noon, ay, and till dewy eve, would we have waited. Just think of our start being graced by the author of "The Adventures of a Phaeton," and we privileged to give him three rousing cheers as our horn sounded. Though grieved to miss him, it was a consolation to know that he had come, and we felt that his spirit was with us and dwelt with us during the entire journey. Many a time the incidents of his charming story came back to us, but I am sorry to record, as a faithful chronicler, that we young people missed one of its most absorbing features—we had no lovers. At least, I am not apprised that any engagements were made upon the journey, although, for my part, I couldn't help falling in love just a tiny bit with the charming young ladies who delighted us with their company.

BRIGHTON, Friday Morning, June 17.

Let us call the roll once more at the door of the Grand Hotel, Brighton, that our history may be complete: Mr. and Miss Beck, London; Mr. and Mrs. Thomas Graham, Wolverhampton; Cousin Maggie Lauder, Dunfermline; dear Emma Franks, Liverpool; Mr. and Mrs. McCargo, Miss Jeannie Johns, Miss Alice French, Benjamin F. Vandevort, Henry Phipps, Jr., G. F. McCandless, Mother and the Scribe. These be the names of the new and delectable order of the Gay Charioteers, who mounted their coach at Brighton and began the long journey to the North Countrie on the day and date aforesaid. And here, O my good friends, let me say that until a man has stood at the door and unexpectedly seen his own four-in-hand drive up before him, the horses—four noble bays—champing the bits, their harness buckles glistening in the sun; the coach spick and span new and as glossy as a mirror, with the coachman on the box and the footman behind; and then, enchanted, has called to his friends, "Come, look, there it is, just as I had pictured it!" and has then seen them mount to their places with beaming faces—until, I say, he has had that experience, don't tell me that he has known the most exquisite sensation in life, for I know he hasn't. It was Izaak Walton, I believe, who when asked what he considered the most thrilling sensation in life, answered that he supposed it was the tug of a thirty-pound salmon. Well, that was not a bad guess. I have taken the largest trout of the season on bonnie Loch Leven, have been drawn over Spirit Lake in Iowa in my skiff for half an hour by a monster pickerel, and have played with the speckled beauties in Dead River. It is glorious; making a hundred thousand is nothing to it; but there's a thrill beyond that, my dear old quaint Izaak. I remember in one of my sweet strolls "ayont the wood mill braes" with a great man, my Uncle Bailie Morrison—and I treasure the memory of these strolls as among the chief of my inheritance—this very question came up. I asked him what he thought the most thrilling thing in life. He mused awhile, as was the Bailie's wont, and I said, "I think I can tell you, Uncle." "What is it then, Andrea?" (Not *Andrew* for the world, mother and the Bailie have the other.) "Well, Uncle, I think that when, in making a speech, one feels himself lifted, as it were, by some divine power into regions beyond himself, in which he seems to soar without effort, and swept by enthusiasm into the expression of some burning truth, which has laid brooding in his soul, throwing policy and prudence to the winds, he feels words whose eloquence surprises himself, burning hot, hissing through him like molten lava coursing the veins, he throws it forth, and panting for breath hears the quick, sharp, explosive roar of his fellow-men in thunder of assent, the precious moment which tells him that the audience is his own, but one soul in it and that his; I think this the supreme moment of life." "Go! Andrea, ye've hit it!" cried the Bailie, and didn't the dark eye sparkle! He had felt this often, had the Bailie; his nephew had only now and then been near enough to imagine the rest.

Mr. Adam Johnston once told me that, though he had heard the most noted orators of Britain, he never yet heard any one whose mastery of a popular audience was as complete as uncle's. Great praise this from such a source; but the head of our family, Uncle Tom, was even more than a natural orator; with all his glowing fire he was characterized by rare sagacity and sound common sense. And how sterling his honesty! All men knew where Tammy Morrison was to be found. A grand Radical, like his father before him, and this nephew after him, who will try, politically speaking at least, never to disgrace the family.

The happiness of giving happiness is far sweeter than the pleasure direct, and I recall no moments of my life in which the rarer pleasure seemed to suffuse my whole heart as when I stood at Brighton and saw my friends take their places that memorable morning. In this variable, fantastic climate of Britain the weather is ever a source of solicitude. What must it have been to me, when a good start was all important! I remember I awoke early that day and wondered whether it was sunny or rainy. If a clear day could have been purchased, it would have been obtained at almost any outlay. I could easily tell our fate by raising the window-blind, but I philosophically decided that it was best to lie still and take what heaven might choose to send us. I should know soon enough. If rain it was, I could not help it; if fair, it was all right. But let me give one suggestion to those who in England are impious enough to ask heaven to change its plans: don't ask for dry weather; always resort to that last extremity when it is "a drizzle-drozzle" you wish. Your supplications are so much more likely to be answered, you know.

There never was a lovelier morning in England than that which greeted me when I pulled up the heavy Venetian blind and gazed on the rippling sea before me, with its hundreds of pretty little sails. I repeated to myself these favorite lines as I stood entranced:

> "The Bridegroom Sea is toying with the shore,
> His wedded bride; and in the fulness of his marriage joy
> He decorates her tawny brow with shells,
> Retires a space to see how fair she looks,
> Then proud runs up to kiss her."

That is what old ocean was doing that happy morning. I saw him at it, and I felt that if all created beings had one mouth I should like to kiss them too.

All seated! Mother next the coachman, and I at her side. The horn sounds, the crowd cheers, and we are off. A mile or two are traversed and there is a unanimous verdict upon one point—this suits us! Finer than we had dreamt! As we pass the pretty villas embossed in flowers and vines and all that makes England the home of happy homes, there comes the sound of increasing exclamations. How pretty! Oh, how beautiful! See, see, the roses! oh the roses! Look at that lawn! How lovely! Enchanting! entrancing! superb! exquisite! Oh, I never saw anything like this in all my life! And then the hum of song—La-*la* LA-LA, Ra-da-*da*-DUM! Yes, it is all true, all we dreamt or imagined and beyond it. And so on we go through Brighton and up the hills to the famous Weald of Sussex.

While we make our first stop to water the horses at the wayside inn, and some of the men as well, for a glass of beer asserts its attractions, let me introduce you to two worthies whose names will occupy important places in our narrative, and dwell in our memories forever; men to whom we are indebted in a large measure for the success of the coaching experiment.

Ladies and gentlemen, this is Perry, Perry our coachman; and what he doesn't know about horses and how to handle them you needn't overtask yourselves trying to learn. And this is Joe —Joey, my lad—footman and coach manager. A good head and an eloquent tongue has Joe. Yes, and a kind heart. There is nothing he can do or think of doing for any of us—and he can do much—that he is not off and doing ere we ask him. "Skid, Joe!"

"Right, Perry!" these talismanic words of our order we heard to-day for the first time. It will be many a long day before they cease to recall to the Charioteers some of the happiest recollections of life. Even as I write I am in English meadows far away and hear them tingling in my ears.

It was soon discovered that no mode of travel could be compared with coaching. By all other modes the views are obstructed by the hedges and walls; upon the top of the coach the eye wanders far and wide,

> "O'er deep waving fields and pastures green,
> With gentle slopes and groves between."

Everything of rural England is seen, and how exquisitely beautiful it all is, this quiet, peaceful, orderly land!

> "The ground's most gentle dimplement
> (As if God's finger touched, but did not press,
> In making England)—such an up and down
> Of verdure; nothing too much up and down,
> A ripple of land, such little hills the sky
> Can stoop to tenderly and the wheat-fields climb;
> Such nooks of valleys lined with orchises,
> Fed full of noises by invisible streams,
> I thought my father's land was worthy too of being Shakespeare's."

I think this extract from Mr. Winter's charming volume expresses the feelings one has amid such scenes better than anything I know of:

"If the beauty of England were merely superficial, it would produce a merely superficial effect. It would cause a passing pleasure, and would be forgotten. It certainly would not—as now in fact it does—inspire a deep, joyous, serene and grateful contentment, and linger in the mind, a gracious and beneficent remembrance. The conquering and lasting potency of it resides not alone in loveliness of expression, but in loveliness of character. Having first greatly blessed the British Islands with the natural advantages of position, climate, soil, and products, nature has wrought out their development and adornment as a necessary consequence of the spirit of their inhabitants. The picturesque variety and pastoral repose of the English landscape spring, in a considerable measure, from the imaginative taste and the affectionate gentleness of the English people. The state of the country, like its social constitution, flows from principles within (which are constantly suggested), and it steadily comforts and nourishes the mind with a sense of kindly feeling, moral rectitude, solidity, and permanence. Thus, in the peculiar beauty of England the ideal is made the actual, is expressed in things more than in words, and in things by which words are transcended. Milton's 'L'Allegro,' fine as it is, is not so fine as the scenery—the crystallized, embodied poetry—out of which it arose. All the delicious rural verse that has been written in England is only the excess and superflux of her own poetic opulence; it has rippled from the hearts of her poets just as the fragrance floats away from her hawthorn hedges. At every step of his progress the pilgrim through English scenes is impressed with this sovereign excellence of the accomplished fact, as contrasted with any words that can be said in its celebration."

The roads are a theme of continual wonder to those who have not before seen England. To say that from end to end of our journey they equalled those of New York Central Park would be to understate the fact. They are equal to the park roads on days when these are at their best, and are neither dry nor dusty. We bowl over them as balls do over billiard-tables. It is a glide rather than a roll, with no sensation of jolting. You could write or read on the coach almost as well as at home. I mean you could if there was any time to waste doing either, and you were not afraid of missing some beautiful picture which would dwell in your memory for years, or Aleck's last joke, or Jeannie's sweet song, Andrew Martin's never-to-be-forgotten lilt, or the Lady Dowager's Scotch ballad pertaining to the district; or what might be even still more likely, if you didn't want to tell a story yourself, or even join in the roaring chorus as we roll along, for truly the exhilarating effect of the triumphant progress is such as to embolden one to do anything. I always liked Artemus Ward, perhaps because I found a point of similarity between him and myself. It was not he but his friend who "was saddest when he sang," as the old song has it. I noticed that my friends were strangely touched when I burst into song. I do not recall an instance when I was encored; but the apparent slight arose probably from a suspicion that if recalled I would have essayed the same song. This is unjust! I have another in reserve for such an occasion, if it ever happen. The words are different, although the tune may be somewhat similar. When I like a tune I stick to it, more or less, and when there are fine touches in several tunes I have been credited with an eclectic disposition. However this may be, there was never time upon our coach for anything which called our eyes and our attention from the rapid succession of pretty cottages, fine flowers, the birds and lowing herds, the grand lights and grander shadows of that uncertain fleecy sky, the luxuriance of the verdure, flowery dells and dewy meads, and the hundred surprising beauties that make England England.

These bind us captive and drive from the mind every thought of anything but the full and intense enjoyment of the present hour; and this comes without thought. Forgetful of the past, regardless of the future, from morn till night, it is one uninterrupted season of pure and unalloyed joyousness. Never were the words of the old Scotch song as timely as now:

"The present moment is our ain,
The neist we never see."

Having got the party fairly started, let me tell you something of our general arrangements for the campaign. The coach, horses, and servants are engaged at a stipulated sum per week, which includes their travelling expenses. We have nothing to do with their bills or arrangements, neither are we in any wise responsible for accidents to the property. Every one is allowed a small hand-bag and a strap package; the former contains necessary articles for daily use, the latter waterproofs, shawls, shoes, etc. The Gay Charioteers march with supplies for one week. The trunks are forwarded every week to the point where we are to spend the succeeding Sunday, so that every Saturday evening we replenish our wardrobe, and at the Sunday evening dinner our ladies appear in grand toilette. In no case did any failure of this plan occur, nor were we ever put to the slightest inconvenience about clothing. Our hotel accommodations were secured by telegraph. Mr. Graham, previous to our start, had engaged these for our first week's stage.

The question of luncheon soon came to the front, for should we be favored with fine weather, much of the poetry and romance of the journey was sure to cluster round the midday halt. It was by a process of natural selection that she who had proved her genius for making salads on many occasions during the voyage should be unanimously appointed to fill the important position of stewardess, and given full and unlimited control of the hampers. Miss French lived up to a well-deserved reputation by surprising us day after day with luncheons far excelling any dinner. Two coaching hampers, very complete affairs, were obtained in London. These the stewardess saw filled at the inn every morning with the best the country could afford, giving this her personal supervision, a labor of love. Harry's sweet tooth led him to many early excursions before breakfast in quest of sweets and flowers for us. Aleck was butler, and upon him we placed implicit reliance, and with excellent reason too, for the essential corkscrew and the use thereof—which may be rated as of prime necessity upon such a tour—and Aleck never failed us as superintendent of the bottles.

It was in obedience to the strictest tenets of our civil service reform association that the most important appointment of all was made with a unanimity which must ever be flattering to the distinguished gentleman who received the highly responsible appointment of general manager. Gardiner had evidently been born for the position. A man does not generally learn until he is forty what he can do to perfection; but there are thirty-two ready to certify that our general manager has not needed to wait so long. If he ever requires backers as the best manager—the very ideal manager of a coaching party—apply within. He had ten days' instruction from a master hand, friend Graham, who resigned office and retired to the shades of private life at Wolverhampton. It was Mr. Graham who arranged all the preliminaries, so that none of us had a thing to do at Brighton but to mount into our seats. He and Gardiner are twins in greatness, and, as far as our party is concerned, neither could be equalled except by the other. Just here let me note, for the peace of mind of any gentleman who may be tempted to try the coaching experiment: *Don't*, unless you have a dear friend with a clear head, an angelic disposition, a great big heart, and the tact essential for governing, who for your sake is willing to relieve you from the cares incident to such a tour—that is, if you expect to enjoy it as a recreation, and have something that forever after will linger in the memory as an adventure in wonderland.

There must always be a tendency toward grouping in a large party: groups of four or five, and in extreme cases a group of two; and especially is this so when married people, cousins, or dear friends are of the company. To prevent anything like this, and insure our being one united party, I asked the gentlemen not to occupy the same seat twice in succession—a rule which gave the ladies a different companion at each meal. This was understood to apply in a general way to our strolls, although in this case the general manager, with rare discretion, winked at many infringements, which insured him grateful constituents of both sexes. Young people should never be held too strictly to such rules, and a chaperon's duties, as we all know, are often most successfully performed by a wise and salutary neglect. Our general manager and even the Lady Dowager were considerate.

We generally started about half-past nine in the morning, half an hour earlier or later as the day's journey was to be long or short; and here let me record, to the credit of all, that not in any instance had we ever to wait for any of the party beyond the five minutes allowed upon all well-managed lines for "variation of watches." The horn sounded, and we were off through the crowds which were usually around the hotel door awaiting the start. Nor even at meals were we less punctual or less mindful of the comfort of others. I had indeed a model party in every way, and in none more praiseworthy than in this, that the Charioteers were always "on time." Jeannie's explanation may have reason in it: "Who wouldn't be ready and waiting to mount the coach! I'd as soon be late, and a good deal sooner, maybe, for my wedding as for meals; there was even a better reason why we were always ready then: we could hardly wait." We did indeed eat like hawks, especially at luncheon—a real boy's hunger—the ravenous gnawing after a day at the sea gathering whilks. I thought this had left me, but that with many another characteristic of glorious youth came once more to make daft callants of us. O those days! those happy, happy days! Can they be brought back once more? Will a second coaching trip do it? I would be off next summer. But one hesitates to put his luck to the test a second time, lest the perfect image of the first be marred. We shall see.

During the evening we had learned the next day's stage—where we were to stay over night, and, what is almost as important, in what pretty nook we were to rest at midday; on the banks of what classic stream or wimpling burn, or in what shady, moss-covered dell. Several people of note in the neighborhood dropped into the inn, as a rule, to see the American coaching party, whose arrival in the village had made as great a stir as if it were the advance show-wagon of Barnum's menagerie. From these the best route and objects of interest to be seen could readily be obtained. The ordnance maps which we carried kept us from trouble about the right roads; not only this, they gave us the name of every estate we passed, and of its owner.

The horses have to be considered in selecting a luncheon-place, which should be near an inn, where they can be baited. This was rarely inconvenient; but upon a few occasions, when the choice spot was in some glen or secluded place, we took oats along, and our horses were none the worse off for nibbling the roadside grass and drinking from the brook. Nor did the party look less like the aristocratic gypsies they felt themselves to be from having their coach standing on the moor or in the glen, and the horses picketed near by, as if we were just the true-born gypsies. And was there ever a band of gypsies happier than we, or freer from care? Didn't we often dash off in a roar:

> "See ! the smoking bowl before us,
> Mark our jovial ragged ring !
> Round and round take up the chorus,
> And in raptures let us sing.
> A fig for those by law protected !
> Liberty's a glorious feast !
> Courts for cowards were erected,
> Churches built to please the priest."

Halt! Ho for luncheon! Steps, Joe. Yes, sir! The committee of two dismount and select the choicest little bit of sward for the table. It is not too warm, still we will not refuse the shade of a noble chestnut or fragrant birk, or the side of a tall hedge, on which lie, in one magnificent bed, masses of honeysuckle, over which nod, upon graceful sprays, hundreds of the prettiest wild roses, and at whose foot grow the foxglove and wandering willie.

It is no easy matter to decide which piece of the velvety lawn is finest; but here come Joe and Perry with armfuls of rugs to the chosen spot. The rugs are spread two lengthwise a few feet apart, and one across at the top and bottom, leaving for the table in the centre the fine clovered turf with buttercups and daisies pied. The ladies have gathered such handfuls of wild flowers! How fresh, how unaffected, and how far beyond the more pretentious bouquets which grace our city dinners! These are Nature's own dear children, fresh from her lap, besprinkled with the dews of heaven, unconscious of their charms. How touchingly beautiful are the wild flowers! real friends are they, close to our hearts, while those of the conservatory stand outside, fashionable acquaintances only.

Give us the wild flowers, and take your prize varieties; for does not even Tennyson (a good deal of a cultivated flower himself) sing thus of the harshest of them all, though to a Scotsman sacred beyond all other vegetation:

> . . . " the stubborn thistle bursting
> Into glossy purples, which outredden
> All voluptuous garden roses."

And in that wonder of our generation, the "Light of Asia," it is no garden beauties who are addressed:

> "' Oh, flowers of the field! Siddârtha said,
> Who turn your tender faces to the sun—
> Glad of the light, and grateful with sweet breath
> Of fragrance and these robes of reverence donned,
> Silver and gold and purple—none of ye
> Miss perfect living, none of ye despoil
> Your happy beauty. . . .
> What secret know ye that ye grow content,
> From time of tender shoot to time of fruit,
> Murmuring such sun-songs from your feathered crowns?'"

You may be sure that while in Scotland old Scotia's dear emblem, and that most graceful of all flowers, the Scottish bluebell, towered over our bouquets, and that round them clustered the others less known to fame.

It was an easy matter to tie the flowers round sticks and press these into the soft lawn, and then there was a table for you—equal it who can! Round this the travellers range themselves upon the rugs, sometimes finding in back to back an excellent support, for they sat long at table ; and see at the head—for it's the head wherever the Queen Dowager sits—mother is comfortably seated upon the smaller of the two hampers. The larger placed on end before her gives her a private table : she has an excellent seat, befitting her dignity. Joe and Perry have put the horses up at the inn, and are back with mugs of foaming ale, bottles of Devonshire cider, lemonade, and pitchers of fresh creamy milk, that all tastes may be suited. The stewardess and her assistants have set table, and now luncheon is ready. No formal grace is necessary, for our hearts have been overflowing with gratitude all the day long for the blessed happiness showered upon us. We owe no man a grudge, harbor no evil, have forgiven all our enemies, if we have any—for we doubt the existence of enemies, being ourselves the enemy of none. Our hearts open to embrace all things, both great and small ; we are only sorry that so much is given to us, so little to many of our more deserving fellow-creatures. Truly, the best grace this, before meat or after !

> "He prayeth best who loveth best
> All things both great and small ;
> For the dear God who loveth us,
> He made and loveth all."

In these days we feel for the Deevil himself, and wish with Burns that he would take a thought and mend ; and, as Howells says, if we had the naming of creation we wouldn't call snakes snakes while coaching.

No one would believe what fearful appetites driving in this climate gives one. Shall we ever feel such tigerish hunger again! but, what is just as important, shall we ever again have such luncheons! "Give me a sixpence," said the beggar to the duke, "for I have nothing." "You lie, you beggar; I'd give a thousand pounds for such an appetite as you've got." Well, ours would have been cheap to you, my lord duke, at double the money. What a roar it caused one day when one of the young ladies was discovered quietly taking the third slice of cold ham. "Well, girls, you must remember I was on the front seat, and had to stand the *brunt* of the weather this morning." Capital! I had been there at her side, and got my extra allowance on the same ground; and those who bore the *brunt* of the weather claimed a great many second and even third allowances during the journey.

Aleck (*Aa*leck, not El-eck, remember), set the table in a roar so often with his funny sayings and doings that it would fill the record were I to recount them, but one comes to mind as I write which was a great hit.

A temperance—no, a total abstinence lady rebuked him once for taking a second or third glass of something, telling him that he should try to conquer his liking for it, and assuring him that if he would only resist the Devil he would flee from him. "I know," said the wag (and with such a comical, good-natured expression), "that is what the good book says, Mrs. ———, but I have generally found that I was the fellow who had *to get*." You couldn't corner Aaleck.

Although we were coaching, it must not be thought that we neglected the pleasures of walking. No, indeed, we had our daily strolls. Sometimes the pedestrians started in advance of the coach from the inn or the luncheon ground, and walked until overtaken, and at other times we would dismount some miles before we reached the end of the day's journey, and walk into the village. This was a favorite plan, as we found by arriving later than the main body our rooms were ready and all the friends in our general sitting-room standing to welcome us.

Hills upon the route were always hailed as giving us an opportunity for a walk or a stroll, and all the sport derivable from a happy party in country lanes. It was early June, quite near enough to

> "The flowery May who from her green lap throws
> The yellow cowslip and the pale primrose,"

and the hundreds of England's wild beauties with

> "quaint enamell'd eyes,
> That on the green turf suck the honeyed showers,
> And purple all the ground with vernal flowers."

We carried perpetual flowering summer with us as we travelled from south to north, plucking the wild roses and the honeysuckles from the hedges near Brighton, never missing their sweet influences, and finding them ready to welcome us at Inverness, as if they had waited till our approach to burst forth in their beauty in kindly greeting of their kinsmen from over the sea. A dancing, laughing welcome did the wild flowers of my native land give to us, God bless them!

On our arrival at the inn for the night, the general manager examined the rooms and assigned them; Joe and Perry handed over the bags to the servants; the party went direct to their general sitting-room, and in a few minutes were taken to their rooms, where all was ready for them. The two American flags were placed upon the mantel of the sitting-room, in which there was always a piano, and we sat down to dinner a happy band.

The long twilight and the gloaming in Scotland gave us two hours after dinner to see the place; and after our return an hour of musical entertainment was generally enjoyed, and we were off to bed to sleep the sound, refreshing sleep of childhood's innocent days. The duties of the general manager, however, required his attendance down stairs; he had to-morrow's route to learn and the landlord or landlady, as the case might be, to see. Some of the male members of the party were not loath to assist in this business, and I have heard many a story of the pranks played —for these good friends Aleck, Graham, and Martin are not unlike Mr. John S. Kennedy's Piper, "Rory Murphy,"

> "Who had of good auld sangs the wale
> To please the wives that brewed good ale;
> He charmed the swats frae cog and pail
> As he cam through Dumbarton."

No doubt the landlord's laugh was ready chorus, and the Gay Charioteers of this department, I make bold to say, tasted most of the "far ben" barrels of every landlord or landlady in their way northward. The question of the weather occurs to every one. "If you have a dry season, it may be done; if a wet one, I doubt it," was the opinion of one of my wisest friends in Britain. We were surprisingly fortunate in this respect. Only one day did we suffer seriously from rain. A gentle shower fell now and then to cool the air and lay the dust, or rather to prevent the dust, and seemingly to recreate vegetation. Who wouldn't bear a shower, if properly supplied with waterproofs and umbrellas, for the fresh glory revealed thereafter. Only a continual downpour for days could have dampened the ardor of the Gay Charioteers. Good coaching weather may be expected in June and July, if one may indulge any weather anticipations in England. After we left the deluge came; nothing but rain was reported during August and September. Strong, thick shoes, one pair in reserve, and overshoes for the ladies, heavy woollen clothing—under and over—a waterproof, an umbrella, and a felt hat that won't spoil—these rendered us almost independent of the weather and prepared us to encounter the worst ever predicted of the British climate; and this is saying a great deal, for the natives do grumble inordinately about it. As I have said, however, our travelling was never put to a severe test. England and Scotland smiled upon the coaching party,. and compelled us all to fall deeply in love with their unrivalled charms. We thought that even in tears this blessed isle must still be enchanting. The same horses (with one exception) took us through from Brighton to Inverness. This has surprised some horsemen here, but little do they know of the roads and climate, nor of Perry's care. The horses were actually in better condition after the journey than when they started. For luncheon, "good my liege, all place a temple and all seasons summer;" but for lodgings and entertainment for man and beast, how did we manage these? Shall we not take our ease in our inn? and shall not mine host of The Garter, ay and mine hostess too, prove the most obliging of people? I do not suppose that it would be possible to find in any other country such delightful inns at every stage of such a journey. Among many pretty objects upon which memory lovingly rests, these little wayside inns stand prominently forward. The very names carry one back to quaint days of old: "The Lamb and Lark," "The Wheat Sheaf," "The Barley Mow." Oh, you fat wight, your inn was in Eastcheap, but in your march through Coventry, when you wouldn't go with your scarecrows, it was to some pretty inn you went, you rogue, with its trailing vines, thatched roof, and pretty garden flower-pots in the windows; and upon such excursions it was, too, that you acquired that love of nature which enabled the master with six words to cover most that was unsavory in your character, and hand you down to generations unborn, shrived and absolved. Dear old boy—whom one would like to have known—for after all you were right, Jack : "If Adam fell in an age of innocency, what was poor Jack Falstaff to do in an age of villainy!" There was something pure and good at bottom of one who left us after life's vanities were o'er playing with flowers and "babbling o' green fields." These country hostelries are redolent of the green fields. It is in such we would take our ease in our inn. The host, hostess, and servants assembled at the door upon our arrival, and welcomed us to their home, as they also do when we leave to bid us God-speed. We mount and drive off with smiles, bows, and wavings of the hands from them; and surely the smiles and good wishes of those who have done so much to promote our comfort over night are no bad salute for us as we blow our horn and start on the fresh dewy mornings upon our day's journey.

The scrupulous care bestowed upon us and our belongings by the innkeepers excited remark. Not one article was lost of the fifty packages, great and small, required by fifteen persons. It was not even practicable to get rid of any trifling article which had served its purpose; old gloves or discarded brushes quietly stowed away in some drawer or other would be handed to us at the next stage, having been sent by express by these careful, honest people. It was a great and interesting occasion, as the reporters say, when the stowed-away pair of old slippers which she had purposely left, were delivered to one of our ladies with a set speech after dinner one evening. Little did she suspect what was contained in the nice package which had been forwarded. Our cast-off things were veritable devil's ducats which would return to plague us.

We all have our special weaknesses as to the articles we leave behind at hotels. Mine is well known; but I smile as I write at the cleverness shown in preventing my lapses during the excursion from coming before the congregation. It was a wary eye which was kept upon forwarded parcels, mark you, and not once was I presented with a left article. The eleventh commandment is, not to be found out.

With these general observations we shall not "leave the subject with you," but, retracing our steps to the hills overlooking Brighton, we shall mount the coach waiting there for us at the King's Cross Inn ; for you remember we dismounted there while the horses were watered for the first time. Ten miles of bewildering pleasure had brought us here ; some of us pushed forward and had our first stroll, but we scattered in a minute, for who could resist the flowers which tempted us at every step ! The roses were just in season : the honeysuckle, ragged robin, meadow sweet, wandering willie, and who can tell how many others whose familiar names are household words. What bouquets we gathered, what exclamations of delight were heard as one mass of beauty after another burst upon our sight ! We began to realize that Paradise lay before us, began to know that we had discovered the rarest plan upon earth for pleasure ; as for duty that was not within our horizon. We scarcely knew there was work to do. An echo of a moan from the weary world we had cast behind was not heard. Divinest melancholy was out of favor ; Il Penseroso was discarded for the time, and L'Allegro, the happier goddess, crowned, bringing in her train—

> "Sport, that wrinkled Care derides,
> And Laughter, holding both his sides ;
> Come, and trip it as you go,
> On the light, fantastic toe."

That does not quite express it, for there was time for momentary pauses now and then, when the heart swelled with gratitude. We were so grateful for being so blessed. It was during this stroll that

Emma came quietly to my side, slipped her arm in mine, and said in that rich, velvety English voice which we all envy her: "Oh, Andrew, when I am to go home you will have to tell me plainly, for indeed I shall never be able to leave this of my own accord. I haven't been as happy since I was a young girl." "Do you really think you could go all the way to Inverness?" "Oh, I could go on this way forever." "All right, my lady, 'check your baggage through,' as we say in Yankeedom;" and never did that woman lose sight of the coach till it was torn away from her at Inverness. We reached Horsham and lunched there at the King's Arms, walked about its principal square, and were off again for Guildford. As we leave the sea the soil becomes richer, and ere we reach Horsham we say, yes, this is England indeed; but I forgot we passed through the Weald of Sussex before reaching Horsham. The cloudy sky cast deep shadows with the sunbeams over the rich, wooded landscape, as no clear blue sky has power to do, and brought to my mind Mrs. Browning's lines:

. . . "my woods in Sussex have some purple shades at gloaming,
Which are worthy of a king in state, or poet in his youth.
   *   *   *   *   *   *   *   *   *   *   *
Oh, the blessed woods of Sussex, I can hear them still around me,
With their leafy tide of greenery still rippling up the wind!"

And many a stately home did we see, fit for her "who spake such good thoughts natural."

Mrs. Browning is said to have written Lady Geraldine in a few hours, lying upon a sofa. This is one of the proofs cited that genius does its work as if by inspiration without great effort. What nonsense! The Victoria Regina bursts into flower in a day; but, look you, a hundred years of quiet, unceasing growth, which stopped not night nor day, was the period of labor preceding the miracle —a hundred years, during all of which the vine drank of the sunshine and the dews. Scott wrote some of his best works in a few weeks, but for a lifetime he never flagged in his work of gathering the fruits of song and story. Burns dashed off "A man's a man for a' that" in a jiffy. Yes, but for how many years were his very heartstrings tingling and his blood boiling at the injustice of hereditary rank! His life is in that song, not a few hours of it.

GUILDFORD, June 17.

The approach to Guildford gives us our first real, perfect English lane—so narrow and so bound in by towering hedgerows worthy the name. Had we met a vehicle at some of the prettiest turns there would have been trouble, for, although the lane is not quite as narrow at the pathway of the auld brig, where two wheelbarrows trembled as they met, yet a four-in-hand upon an English lane requires a clear track. Vegetation near Guildford is luxuriant enough to meet our expectations of England. It was at the White Lion we halted, and here came our first experience of quarters for the night. The first dinner en route was a decided success in our fine sitting-room, the American flags, brought into requisition for the first time to decorate the mantel, bringing to all sweet memories of home.

We had done our first day's coaching, and a long day at that, and looking back it is amusing to remember how anxiously I awaited the reports of the ladies of our party; for it was not without grave apprehension that some must fall by the wayside, as it were, as we journeyed on. One who had tried coaching upon this side had informed me that few ladies could stand it; but it was very evident that the spirits and appetites of ours were entirely satisfactory, and they all laughed at the idea that they could not go on forever. Mother was quite as fresh as any. It was a shame that general orders consigned to bed at an early hour two of the ladies thought least robust, while the others walked about the suburbs of Guildford until late. I recollect we stood in the thickening twilight in front of an ivy-clad residence for some time, and asked each other if anything so exquisite had ever been seen, so full of rest, of home. The next morning all were fresh and happy, without a trace of fatigue—full of yesterday, and quite sure that no other day could equal it. But this was often said: many and many a day was voted the finest yet, only to be eclipsed in its turn by a later, till at last an effort to name our best day led to twenty selections, and ended in the general conclusion that it was impossible to say which had crowded within its hours the rarest treat, for none had all the finest, neither did any lack something of the best. But there is one point upon which a unanimous verdict can always be had from the Gay Charioteers, that to such days in the mass none but themselves can be their parallel.

I ran into a book-shop in the morning and obtained a local guide-book, that I might cull for you the proper quotations therefrom. It consists of 148 pages, mostly given up to notices of the titled people who visited the old town long ago; but who cares about them? Here, however, is something of more interest than all those nobodies. Cobbett says of Guildford, in his "Rural Rides":

"I, who have seen so many towns, think this the prettiest and most happy-looking I ever saw in my life." There's praise for you! But, then, he had never seen Dunfermline. Here is a characteristic touch of that rare, horse-sense kind of a man. He is enraptured over the vale of Chilworth.

"Here, in this tranquil spot, where the nightingales are to be heard earlier and later in the year than in any other part of England, where the first budding of the trees is seen in the spring, where no rigor of seasons can ever be felt, where everything seems framed for precluding the very thought of wickedness—this has the devil fixed on as one of his seats of his grand manufactory, and perverse and even ungrateful man not only lends his aid, but lends it cheerfully."

Since these days, friend Cobbett, the devil has much enlarged his business in gunpowder and banknotes, of which you complain. He was only making a start when you wrote. The development of manufactures in America (under a judicious tariff, be it reverently spoken), amazing as it has been, and carried on as a rule by the saints, is slow work compared with what his satanic majesty has been doing in these two departments. We must bestir ourselves betimes.

You remember Artemus Ward's encounter with the colporteur. After a long, dusty day's journey, arriving at the hotel, he applied to the barkeeper for a mint-julep, and just as Artemus was raising the tempting draught to his lips, a hand was laid upon his arm and the operation arrested. The missionary in embryo said in a kind of sepulchral tone, for he was only a beginner and had not yet reached that true professional voice which comes only after years of exhortation : " My friend, look not upon the wine when it is red. It stingeth like a serpent and it biteth as an adder." " Guess not, stranger," replied Artemus, " not if you put sugar in it."

It is just so with bank-notes, friend Cobbett. They don't bite worth a cent, neither do they sting, if you have government bonds behind them. But this was not understood in your day.

There is a funny thing in this guide-book. " There also resides Mr. Martin Farquhar Tupper, the author of 'Proverbial Philosophy,' etc. He has eulogized the scene around as follows :" Then come two pages of Tupper. I naturally looked to see the name of the author of the book, but none was given. Such modesty ! But I think the case a clear one, for who but Tupper would quote Tupper ! " Sir," said Johnson to Bossy, " Sir, I never did the man an injury in my life, and yet he would persist in reading his tragedy to me." Here's the concluding quotation from the guide-book of Guildford, and I promise not to quote much more from any similar source.

Cobbett says that in Albury Park he saw some plants of the " American cranberry, which not only grow here, but bear fruit, and therefore it is clear that they may be cultivated with great ease in this country." And so they have been and are. Potatoes, tomatoes, and cranberries—look at the great blessings America has bestowed upon the "author of her being;" and what won't grow in the rain and fog, doesn't she grow for her and send over by every steamer, from canvas-back ducks to Newtown pippins! At dinner-tables in England, nowadays, to the usual grace, "O Lord! for what we are about to receive make us truly thankful," there should be added, "and render us truly grateful to our big son Jonathan."

One could settle down at the White Lion in Guildford, and spend a month, at least, visiting every day fresh objects of interest, and I have no doubt becoming day by day more charmed with the life he was leading. In every direction historical scenes, crowded full of instructive stories of the past, invite us; and yet to-morrow morning the horn will sound, and we shall be off, reluctantly saying to ourselves, we must return some day when we have leisure, and wander in and around, absorb and moralize. This rapid survey is only to show us what we can do hereafter. A summer to each county would not be too much, and here are eight hundred miles from sea to firth to be rushed over in seven weeks. Guildford, farewell!—on "to fresh fields and pastures new." During our second day's stage we learned the valuable lesson that we should not attempt to coach through England without having the ordnance survey maps, and paying close attention to them. In this part of the country, so near to monster London, the roads and lanes are innumerable, and run here, there, and everywhere. You can reach any point by many different roads. Guide-posts have a dozen names upon them. We did some sailing out of our course to-day, and found many charming spots not down in the chart, which the straight line would have caused us to miss; but it was late ere Windsor's towers made their appearance. The day was not long enough for us, long as it was, but the fifty miles we are said to have traversed were quite enough for the horses. But next day would be Sunday, we said, and they had a long rest to look forward to at Windsor.

WINDSOR, June 18-20.

Upon reaching the forest, general manager Graham insisted that the chief should take the reins and drive his party through the royal domain. This was my first trial as a whip of a four-in-hand, and not a very successful one either. It's easy enough to handle the ribbons, but how to do this and spare a hand for the whip troubles one. As Josh Billings remarks in the case of religion, "It's easy enough to get religion, but to hold on to it is what bothers a fellow. A good grip is here worth more than rubies." I had not the grip for the whip, but it did give me a rare pleasure when I got a moment or two now and then (when Perry held the whip), to think that I was privileged to drive my friends in style up to Her Majesty's very door at Windsor. Only to the door, for that good woman was not at home, but in bonnie Scotland, sensible lady! As we were en route ourselves, we were quite in the fashion. Some of her republican subjects were quite disappointed at not getting a glimpse of her during the tour.

The drive through the grounds gave to some of our party their first sight of an English park, and I am sure the impression it made upon them will never be effaced.

Windsor at last, a late dinner and a stroll through the quaint town, the castle towering over all in the cloudy night, and we are off to bed, but not before we had enjoyed an hour of the wildest frolic, though tired and sleepy after the long drive. We laughed until our sides ached, but how vain to attempt to describe the fun! To detail the trifles light as air which kept us in a roar during our excursion is like offering you stale champagne. No, no, gone forever are those rare nothings which were so delicious when fresh; but, for the benefit of the members of the Circle, I'll just say "Poole." It was a happy thought to put Gardiner's suit of new clothes in Davie's package and await results. We had all ordered travelling suits in London, and when they arrived we all began to try them on at once. Davie's disappointment at getting an odd-looking suit fancied by Gardiner was so genuine! But such a perfect fit, though a mistake, maybe, as to material; and then, when he tried his own suit, what a misfit it was! The climax: "David, if you are going to"—but this is too much! The tears are rolling down my cheeks once more as I picture that wild scene.

We heard the chimes at midnight, and then to bed. Windsor is nothing unless royal. It is all over royal, although Her Majesty was absent. But the Prince of Wales was there, and a greater than he— Mr. Gladstone—had run down from muggy London to refresh his faded energies by communing with nature. It is said that his friends are alarmed at his haggard appearance toward the close of each week;

but he spends Saturday and Sunday in the country, and returns on Monday to surprise them at the change. Ah! he has found the kindest, truest nurse, for he knows—

> . . . "that Nature never did betray
> The heart that loved her ; 'tis her privilege,
> Through all the years of this our life, to lead
> From joy to joy : for she can so inform
> The mind that is within us, so impress
> With quietness and beauty, and so feed
> With lofty thoughts, that neither evil tongues,
> Rash judgments, nor the sneers of selfish men,
> Her greetings where no kindness is, nor all
> The dreary intercourse of daily life,
> Shall e'er prevail against us, or disturb
> Our cheerful faith, that all which we behold
> Is full of blessings."

Mr. Gladstone's fresh appearance Monday mornings gratifies his friends, and I will believe pleases even his opponents, for such a man can have no ill-wishers, surely. When Confucius had determined to behead the emperor's corrupt brother, his counsellors endeavored to dissuade him, from a just fear that the criminal's friends would rise and avenge his death. "Friends!" said the sage, "such a character may have adherents, but friends never."

The result proved his wisdom. No revolt came, though Confucius stood by to see justice done, refusing to listen to the petition of the emperor for his own brother's life. In like manner, Mr. Gladstone may have opponents—enemies never. All Englishmen must in their hearts honor the man who is a credit to the race. By the way, he's Scotch, let me note, and never fails to bear in mind and to mention this special cause for thankfulness. I suspect that this fact has not a little to do with the intense enthusiasm of Scotland for him. We are a queer lot, up in the North Countrie, and he is our ain bairn. Blood is thicker than water everywhere, but in no part of this world is it so *very much thicker* as beyond the Tweed.

We attended church at Windsor and saw the great man and the other come to the door together. There the former stopped and the other walked up the aisle, causing a flutter in the congregation. Mr. Gladstone followed at a respectful distance, and took his seat several pews behind. How absurd you are, my young lady republican! Can you not understand? One is only the leading man in the empire—a man who, in a fifty years' tussle with the foremost statesmen of the age, has won the crown both for attainments and character; but the other, bless your ignorant little head!—he is a prince.

Well, if he is, he has never done anything, you say. You are mistaken here again, miss. He has shot poor tame pigeons from a trap, many a time, like a man; has even killed a pig, for they told me in India how they placed him upon a platform in a tree, out of harm's way, and then drove the pig past, and he actually hit it. My dear girl, I'll lay two to one that Gladstone would have missed it; and if the prince were to challenge him to a pigeon-match, he would turn away chicken-hearted. Truly, the prince is the right man of the two, you see, for a cultured, civilized people to prefer and make the fountain of honor—King of England and *Emperor* (of India) too—a bad word this and un-English. The prince is the highest product of this people, else they would never elevate him above all others. Go to; you talk like a green girl.

In the afternoon we attended St. George's Chapel. In one of the stalls we saw again that sadly noble lion-face—no one ever mistakes Gladstone. He sat wrapped in the deepest meditation. He is very pale, haggard, and careworn—the weight of empire upon him!

> "I tell thee, scorner of these whitening hairs,
> When this snow melteth there shall come a flood."

I could not help applying to him Milton's lines:

> . . . " with grave
> Aspect he rose, and in his rising seem'd
> A pillar of state: deep on his front engraven
> Deliberation sat and public care;
> And princely counsel in his face yet shone,
> Majestic though in ruin."

He has work to do yet. If he only were fifty instead of seventy odd! Well, God bless him for what he has done; may he rule England long!

A memorable event occurred at Windsor, Sunday, June 19th—my mother reached her seventy-first year. At breakfast Mr. Beck rose, and addressing himself to her, made one of the sweetest, prettiest speeches I ever heard. He presented to her an exquisite silver cup, ornamented with birds and flowers, and inscribed: "Presented to Mrs. Margaret Carnegie, at Windsor, by the members of the coaching-party, upon her seventy-first birthday." Mr. Beck's reference to mother's intense love of nature in all her glorious forms, from the tiny gowan to the extended landscape, was most appropriate.

Mother and I were completely surprised; and

when Mr. Beck concluded, I was about to rise and respond, but a slight motion from her majesty apprized me that she preferred to reply in person. Well, I thought I was the speech-maker for the family. I wonder what that woman will do next! But she acquitted herself grandly. Her speech was a gem; she is the orator of the family, after all (Mem. —It was so short). After thanking her dear friends, she said:

"I can only wish that you may all have as good health, as complete command of all your faculties, and enjoy flowers and birds and all things of nature as much as I do at seventy-one." Here the voice trembled. There were not many dry eyes. The quiver ran through the party, and without another word mother sat slowly down. I was very, very proud of that seventy-year old (I am often that), and deeply moved, as she was, by this touching evidence of the regard of the coaching party for her.

This incident led to some funny stories about presentation speeches. Upon a recent occasion, not far from Paisley, Aggie told us, a worthy deacon had been selected to present a robe to the minister. The church was crowded, and the recipient stood expectantly at the foot of the pulpit, surrounded by the members of his family. Amid breathless silence the committee entered and marched up the aisle, headed by the deacon bearing the gift in his extended arms. On reaching the pulpit a stand was made, but never a word came from the deacon, down whose brow the perspiration rolled in great drops. He was in a daze, but a touch from one of the committee brought him back to something like a realizing sense of his position, and he stammered out, as he handed the robe to the minister:

> "Mr. Broon,
> Here's the goon."

You need not laugh. It is not likely that you could make as good a speech, which, I'll wager, is far better than the one over which he had spent sleepless nights, but which providentially left him at the critical moment.

Windsor, seen from any direction at a distance, is *par excellence* the castle—a truly royal residence; but, seen closely, it loses the grand and sinks into something of prettiness. It is no longer commanding, and is insignificant in comparison with the true castles of the north. The glamour flies when you begin to analyze. Royalty's famous abode should be looked at as royalty itself should be—at a safe distance.

Service at St. George's Chapel will not soon be forgotten by our party. The stalls of the Knights of the Garter, over the canopies of which hang their swords and mantles surmounted by their crests and armorial bearings, carry one far back into the days of chivalry. One stall arrested and held my attention—that of the Earl of Beaconsfield. When I was not gazing at Gladstone's face, I was moralizing upon the last Knight of the Garter, whose flag still floats above the stall. Disraeli won the blue ribbon about as worthily as most men, and by much the same means—he flattered the monarch. But there is this to be said of him: he had brains and made himself.

What a commentary upon pride of birth, the flag of the poor literary adventurer floating beside that of my lord duke's! It pleased me much to see it. How that man must have chuckled as he bowed his way among his dupes, from Her Majesty to Salisbury, and passed the radical extension of the suffrage that doomed hereditary privilege to speedy extinction. But where will imperialism get such another leader, after all? It has not found him yet.

"What is that up there?" asked one of our party. "The royal box, miss." Were we really at the opera, then? A royal box in church for the worship of God! Did you ever hear anything like that! There is a royal staircase, too. Why not? You would not have royalty on an equality with us, would you, even if we are all alike miserable sinners and engaged in the worship of that God who is no respecter of persons.

"Well, I think this is awful," said one of the party. "I don't believe the good Queen would go to church in this way, if she only thought of it. Our President and family have their pew just like the rest of us." Our English members were equally surprised that the American should see anything shocking in the practice, and the ladies fought out the matter between themselves, the Americans insisting that the Queen should attend worship as other poor sinners do, since all are equal in God's eyes; and the English saying little, but evidently harboring the idea that even in heaven special accommodations would probably be found reserved for royalty, with maybe a special staircase to ascend by. Early education and inherited tendencies account for much.

The staircase question led to the story that the Marquis of Lorne was not allowed to enter some performance by the same stair with his wife. The American was up at this. "If I had a husband, and he couldn't come with me, I wouldn't go." This made an end of the discussion, for the English young lady's eyes told plainly of her secret vow that wherever she went —·— must go too. All were agreed on this point; but on the general question it was a drawn battle, the one side declaring that if· they were men they would not have a princess for a wife under any circumstances, and the other insisting that, if they were princesses, they would not have anybody but a prince for a husband.

Monday was another thoroughly English day. The silver Thames glistened in the sun. The castle towered in all its majesty, vivified by the meteor flag which fluttered in the breeze. The grounds of Eton were crowded with nice-looking English boys as we passed. Many of us walked down the steep hill and far into the country in advance of the coach, and felt once more that a fine day in the south of England was perfection indeed. The sun here reminds one of the cup that cheers, but does not inebriate: its rays cheer, but never scorch. You could not tell whether, if there were to be any change, you would prefer it to be a shade cooler or a shade warmer.

Stoke Pogis is a few miles out of our direct road, but who would miss that, even were the detour double what the ordnance survey makes it. Besides, had not Miss Whitfield, a stay-at-home, told us that one of the happiest days of her life was that spent in making a pilgrimage to the shrine of the poet. Gray's was the first shrine at which we stopped to worship, and the beauty, the stillness, the peace of that low, quaint, ivy-covered church, and its old-fashioned graveyard, sank into our hearts. Surely no one could revive memories more sweetly English than he who gave us the Elegy. Some lines, and even verses of that gem, will endure, it may safely be predicted, as long as anything English does, and that is saying much. We found just such a churchyard as seemed suited to the ode. Gray is fortunate in his resting-place. Earth has no prettier, calmer spot to give her child than this. It is the very ideal God's acre. The little church too is perfect. How fine is Gray's inscription upon his mother's tomb! I avoid cemeteries whenever possible, but this seemed more like a place where one revisits those he has once known than that where, alas! he must mourn those lost forever. Gray's voice—the voice of one that is still, even the touch of the vanished hand, these seemed to be found there, for after our visit the poet was closer to me than he had ever been before. It is not thus with such as we have known and loved in the flesh—their graves let us silently avoid. He whom you seek is not here; but the great dead whom we have known only through their souls do come closer to us as we stand over their graves. The flesh we have known has become spiritualized; the spirits we have known become in a measure materialized, and I felt I had a firmer hold upon Gray from having stood over his dust.

Here is the inscription he put upon his mother's grave:

" Dorothy Gray.
The careful, tender mother of many children, one of whom alone had the misfortune to survive her."

The touch in the last words, "the misfortune to survive her!"—Carlyle's words upon his wife's tomb recur to me:

"And he feels that the light of his life has gone out."

These were men wailing for women. I cannot believe but that there are many women who would prefer to share the fate of men who die. There *is* such love on earth. Sujâtas are not confined to India. As she says:

"But if Death called Senáni, I should mount
The pile and lay that dear head in my lap.
My daily way, rejoicing when the torch
Lit the quick flame and rolled the choking smoke.
For it is written, if an Indian wife
Die so, her love shall give her husband's soul
For every hair upon her head, a crore
Of years in Swerza."

I think I know women who would esteem it a mercy to be allowed to pass away with *him*, if the Eternal had not set his "canon 'gainst self-slaughter." This prohibition the Indian wots not of.

Upon Gray's own tomb there is inscribed:

"One morn I missed him on the accustomed hill,
Along the heath, and near his favorite tree;
Another came, nor yet beside the rill,
Nor up the lawn, nor at the wood was he."

One perfect gem outweighs a thousand mediocre performances and makes its creator immortal. The world has not a second Gray's Elegy among all its treasures. Nor is it likely to have. We found you still in your accustomed place.

Our luncheon was to be upon the banks of the

Thames to-day, the old Swan Inn, where the stone bridge crosses the stream, being our base of supplies ; but ere this was reached what a lovely picture was ours between Stoke Pogis and the Swan ! All that has been sung or written about the valley of the Thames is found to be more than deserved. The silver stream flows gently through the valley, the fertile land rises gradually on both sides, enabling us to get extensive views from the top of the coach. Our road lies over tolerably high ground some distance from the river. Such perfect quiet, homelike, luxuriant beauty is to be seen nowhere but in England. It is not possible for the elements to be combined to produce a more pleasing picture ; and now, after seeing all else between Brighton and Inverness that lay upon our line, we return to the region of Streatley and Maple Durham, and award them the palm as the finest thoroughly English landscape.

We say to the valley of the Thames what the Eastern poet said to the Vale of Cashmere, which is not half so pretty :

"If there be a paradise upon earth,
It is here, it is here."

The old Swan proved to be, both in structure and location, a fit component part of the sylvan scene around. There ran the Thames in limpid purity, a picturesque stone bridge overhanging it, and the roadside inn within a few yards of the grassy bank.

The rugs were laid under a chestnut tree, and our first picnic luncheon spread on the buttercups and daisies. Swallows skimmed the water, bees hummed above us—but stop ! listen ! what's that, and where ?

Our first skylark singing at heaven's gate! Davie and Ben and Jeannie and Alice, and all who heard this never-to-be-forgotten song for the first time were up and on their feet in an instant; but the tiny songster which was then filling the azure vault with music was nowhere to be seen. It's worth an Atlantic voyage to hear a skylark for the first time. Even luncheon was neglected for a time, hungry as we were, that we might if possible catch a glimpse of the warbler. The flood of song poured forth as we stood rapt awaiting the descent of the messenger from heaven. At last a small black speck came into sight. He is so little to see—so great to hear!

I know three fine things about the famous songster:

> "In the golden lightning
> Of the sunken sun,
> O'er which clouds are bright'ning,
> Thou dost float and run,
> Like an unbodied joy whose race is just begun."

An "unbodied joy"! that's a hit, surely!

Here is Browning on the thrush, which I think should be to the lark:

> "He sings each song twice over,
> Lest you should think he never could recapture
> The first fine careless rapture."

The third is just thrown in by the prodigal hand of genius in a poem not to a lark but to a daisy:

> "Alas! it's no thy neebor sweet,
> The bonnie lark, companion meet,
> Bending thee 'mang the dewy weet,
>   Wi' speckl'd breast,
> When upward springing, blithe, to greet
>   The purpling east."

And now I remember Shakespeare has his say too about the lark—what is it in England he has not his say about? or in all the world for that matter; and how much and how many things has he rendered it the highest wisdom for man to keep silent about after he has said his say, holding their peace forever.

A row upon the silver Thames after luncheon, and we are off again for Reading, where we are to rest over night at the Queen's. Reading has a pretty, new park and interesting ruins within its boundaries which we visited before dinner. A pretty lawn in the rear of our hotel gave us an opportunity for a game at lawn tennis in the twilight after dinner, and in the morning we were off for Oxford.

The editorial in the Reading paper that morning upon emigration struck me as going to the root of the matter. Here is the concluding paragraph:

"Already the expanding and prospering industries of the New World are throwing an ominous shadow across the Old World and are affecting some of its habits and practices. But over and above and beyond all these, the free thought, the liberty of action, the calm independence and the sense of the dignity of man as man, and the perfect equality of all before the law and in the eye of the constitution now existing in America, are developing a race of men who, through correspondence with home relations, the intercourse of free travel, the transaction of business, and the free, outspoken language of the press, are gradually disintegrating the yet strong conservative forces of European society, and thus preparing the downfall of the monarchical, aristocratic, military, and ecclesiastic systems which shackle and strangle the people of the Old World. These thoughts seem to me to convey the meaning of the great exodus now going on, and he is a wise statesman who reads the lesson aright."

There's a man after my own heart. He grasps the subject.

The editor tells one of the several causes of the exodus which is embracing many of the most valuable citizens of the old lands where class distinctions still linger. Man longs not only to be free but to be equal, if he has much manhood in him; and that America is the home for such men, numbers of the best are fast finding out. But England will soon march forward; she is not going to rest behind very long. There will soon be no political advantages here over England for the masses.

Some of us walked ahead of the coach for several miles, and I had a chat with a man whom we met. He was a rough carpenter and his wages were sixteen shillings per week ($4). A laborer gets eleven shillings (not $2.75), but some "good masters" pay thirteen to fourteen shillings ($3.25 to $3.50), and give their men four or five pounds of beef at Christmas. Food is bacon and tea, which are cheap—but no beef. Men's wages have not advanced much for many years (I should think not!), but women's have. An ordinary woman for field work can get one shilling per day (24 cents); a short time ago ninepence (18 cents) was the highest amount paid. Is it not cheering to find poor women getting an advance? But think what their condition still is, when one shilling per day is considered good pay! I asked whether employers did not board the workers in addition to paying these wages, but he assured me they did not. This is Southern England and these are agricultural laborers, but the wages seem distressingly low even as compared with British wages in general. The new system of education and the coming extension of the suffrage to the counties will soon work a change among these poor people. They will not rest content crowding each other down thus to a pittance when they can read and write and vote. Thank fortune for this.

Our ladies were unusually gay in their decorations to-day, with bunches of wild flowers on their breasts and hats crowned with poppies and roses. They decked mother out until she looked as if she were ready to play Ophelia. Their smiles too were as pretty as their flowers. What an embodied joy bright, happy ladies are under all conditions, and how absolutely essential for a coaching party! Was it not Johnson's idea of happiness to drive in a gig with a pretty woman? He wasn't much of a muff! If anything could have kept him in good humor, this would have done it. If he could have been on top of a coach with a bevy of them, not even he could have said a rude thing.

Oxford was reached before the sun went down. Its towers were seen for miles—Magdalen, Baliol, Christ Church, and other familiar names. We cross the pretty little Isis, marvelling at every step, and drive up the High Street to the Clarendon.

To-morrow is to be commencement day, and only a few rooms are to be had in the hotel, but we were distributed very comfortably among houses in the neighborhood. Several hours before dinner were delightfully spent in a grand round of the colleges. We peeped into the great quads, walked the cloisters, and got into all kinds of queer old-fashioned places. But the stroll along the Isis, and past Magdalen Tower, and up the long walk—that was the grand finish! We pardon Wolsey his greed of getting, he was so princely in giving. To the man who did so much for Oxford much may be forgiven.

OXFORD, June 21.

This morning was devoted to visiting the principal colleges more in detail, and also to the ascent of the tower of the Sheldonian Theatre, which no one should ever miss doing. Below us lay the city of palaces, for such it seems, palaces of the right kind too—not for idle kings or princes to riot in, and corrupt society by their bad example, but for those who "scorn delights and live laborious days."

Our Cambridge member, Mr. Beck, tells us it does not cost more than £200 ($1000) per annum for a student here. This seems very cheap. The tariff which we saw in one of the halls gave us a laugh :

"Commons.

Mutton, long, 11*d*.
   do. short, 9*d*.
   do. half, 7*d*."

The long and the half we could understand, but how do they manage the short? This must be a kind of medium portion for fellows whose appetites are only so-so. You see how fine things are cut even in Oxford. Our party thought if the students were coaching there would be little occasion for them to know anything of either short or half. At least we were all in for long commons at eleven pence.

We drove past the martyrs' memorial, Latimer and Ridley's. Cranmer does not deserve to be named with them. A visit to such a monument always does me good, for it enables me to say to those who doubt the real advancement of mankind: Now look at this, and think for what these grand men were burnt! Is it conceivable that good, sterling men shall ever again be called upon in England to die for opinion's sake! That Cranmer wrote and advocated the right and necessity of putting to death those who differed from him, and therefore that he met the fate he considered it right to mete to others, shows what all parties held in those dark days. I claim that the world has made a distinct and permanent advance in this department which in no revolving circle of human affairs is ever to be lost. The persecution of the Rev. Mr. Green, of Professor Robertson Smith, and of Bishop Colenso in the present day proves, no doubt, that there is much yet to be done ere we can be very proud of our progress; but these are the worst of to-day's persecutions and could occur only in England and Scotland. There is a long gap between them and burning at the stake! Grand old Latimer was prophetic when he called out to his colleague: " Be of good comfort and play the man; we shall this day light such a candle by God's grace as I trust shall never be put out!"

I think it certain that the candle will never again

be put out. The bigots of to-day can only annoy in Britain. In other English-speaking communities even that power has passed away, and persecution for opinion's sake is unknown.

We left Oxford with just a sprinkle of rain falling, but we had scarcely got fairly out of the city when it ceased and left the charming landscape lovelier than ever. Banbury Cross was our destination, and on our route lay magnificent Blenheim, the estate given by the nation to the Duke of Marlborough. See what the nations do for the most successful murderers of their fellows! and how insignificant have ever been the rewards of those who preserve, improve, or discover—for a Marlborough or a Wellington a fortune, for a Howard or a Wilberforce a pittance. It is only in heathen China that the statesman, the man of letters, heads the list. No military officer, however successful as a destroyer, can ever reach the highest rank there, for with them the victories of peace are more renowned than those of war ; that is reserved for the men who know—the Gladstones and the Disraelis, the Darwins and the Huxleys, the Arnolds and the Ruskins. It is only in civilized countries that the first honors are given to butchers.

Blenheim is superb, grand, and broad enough to satisfy princely tastes. And that noble library ! As we walked through it we felt subdued as if in the presence of the gods of ages past, for a worthy collection of great books ever breathes forth the influence of kings dead yet present, of

> " Those dead but sceptred sovereigns
> Whose spirits still rule us from their urns."

And to think that this library, in whose treasures we revelled, reverently taking one old tome after another in our hands, has since then been sold by auction! Degenerate wretch! but one descended from Marlborough can scarcely be called degenerate. You may not even be responsible for what seems like family dishonor; some previous heir may have rendered the sale necessary; but the dispersion of such treasures as these must surely open the eyes of good men in England to the folly of maintaining hereditary rank and privilege. Perhaps, however, the noble owner had no more use for his books than the lord whose library Burns was privileged to see, which showed no evidences of usage. The bard wrote in a volume of Shakespeare he took up:

> "Through and through the inspired leaves,
> Ye maggots, make your windings;
> But oh! respect his lordship's taste
> And spare his golden bindings."

With many notable exceptions, the aristocracy of Britain took its rise from bad men who did the dirty work of miserable kings, and from women who were even worse than their lords. It seems hastening to an end in a manner strictly in accordance with its birth. Even Englishmen will soon become satisfied that no man should be born to honors, but that these should be reserved for those who merit them. But what kind of fruit could be expected from the tree of privilege? Its roots lie in injustice, and not the least of its evils are those inflicted upon such as are born under its shadow. The young peer who succeeds in making somebody of himself does so in spite of a vicious system, and is entitled to infinite praise; but though our race is slow to learn, the people hear a wee bird singing these stirring days, and they begin to like the song. The days of rank are numbered.

BANBURY, June 22.

Banbury Cross came into sight about five o'clock, and few of us were so far away in years or feeling from the days of childhood as not to remember the nursery rhyme which was repeated as we drove past the Cross; but it is an elaborate Gothic cross, looking as new and modern as if Gilbert Scott had put the finishing touches to it but yesterday, and the charm was gone. I like new political institutions for my native land, but prefer the old historical structures. The besom of destruction should have spared Banbury Cross. I hope the old Cross has been put away in some museum or other safe place out of the weather. We must see about this on our next visit.

Banbury has the celebrated works of my friend, Mr. Samuelson, M.P.; and before dinner I walked out to see them, and if possible to learn something of Mr. Samuelson's whereabouts. Upon returning to the hotel I found that he was at that moment occupying the sitting-room adjoining ours. We had an evening's talk and compared notes as brother manufacturers. If England and America are drawing more closely together politically, it is also true that the manufacturers of the two countries have nearly the same problems to settle. Mr. Samuelson was deep in railway discriminations and laboring with a parliamentary commission to effect changes, or rather, as he would put it, to obtain justice. I gave him an account of our plans, our failures, and our successes, of which he took note. This much I am bound to say for my former colleagues upon this side (for before I reformed I was a railway manager), that the manufacturers of Britain have wrongs of which we know nothing here, though ours are bad enough. I add the last sentence lest Messrs. Vanderbilt, Roberts, Cassatt, and the Garretts (father and son), might receive a wrong impression from the previous admission; for these are the gentlemen upon whom our fortunes hang.

Banbury is a very pretty, clean, well-to-do town, and evidently prosperous, but our ladies have the removal of the old Cross down in their note-books as a serious charge against its reverence; for what makes Banbury a household word in every nursery?

There is much discussion this morning as to the best route to take, there is so much to tempt us on either of several ways. Shall we go by Compton Verney (there is a pretty English name for you), Wellesbourn, and Hastings? or shall we take our way through Broughton Castle, Tadmarton, Scoalcliffe, Compton Wynyate, and Oxhill? In one way Wroxton Abbey, one of the real genuine baronial abbeys, if one may say so, and Edgehill. Surely no good Republican would miss that! But on the other route we shall see the stronghold of Lord Saye and Sele, older yet than Wroxton, and Compton Wynyate, older and finer than all—"a noble wreck in ruinous perfection," and a third route still finer than either as far as scenery is concerned. Such is this treasure house, this crowded grand old England, whose every mile boasts such attractions to win our love.

> " Look where we may, we cannot err
> In this delicious region—change of place
> Producing change of beauty—ever new."

We chose the first route, and whatever the others might have proved we are satisfied, for it is unanimously decided that in Wroxton Abbey we have seen our most interesting structure. It is early English indeed! Blenheim and Windsor are larger, but not for a dozen of either would we exchange this grand old abbey. We revelled in its quaint irregular chambers. James the First slept in that bed, George the Fourth in that; this quilt is the work of Mary Queen of Scots—there is her name; Queen Elizabeth occupied this chamber upon her royal progress, and King William this. Then the genuine old pictures, although in this department Blenheim stands unrivalled. Marlborough knew the adage that "to the victor belongs the spoils," and acted upon it too, for he had rare opportunities abroad to gather treasures. But for a realization of your most picturesque ideal of a great old English house, betake yourselves to Wroxton Abbey. Its little chapel, rich in very old oak carving, is in itself worth a journey to see.

We lunched off deal tables and drank home-brewed ale in the tap-room of the Holcroft Inn, a queer old place, but we had a jolly time amid every kind of thing that carried us back to the England of

past centuries. Beyond Holcroft we came suddenly
upon the grandest and most extensive view by far
that had yet rejoiced us. We were rolling along
absorbed in deep admiration of the fertile land which
spread out before us on both sides of the road, and
extolling the never-ceasing peacefulness and quiet
charm of England, when, on passing through a cut,
a wide and varied panorama lay stretched at our feet.
A dozen picturesque villages and hamlets were in
sight, and by the aid of our field-glass a dozen more
were brought within range. The spires of the
churches, the poplars, the hedgerows, the woods, the
gently undulating land apparently giving forth its
luxuriant harvest with such ease and pleasure, all
these made up such a picture as we could not leave.
We ordered the coach to go on and wait at the foot
of the hill until we had feasted ourselves with the
view. We lay upon the face of the hill and gazed
on Arcadia smiling below. Very soon some of the
neighboring residents came, for one is never long
without human company in crowded England; and
we found that we were indeed upon sacred ground.
This was Edgehill. Shade of Cromwell! was it here
you showed what man can do for a great cause when
moved to take up arms, not for hire nor for fame,
but for duty, stern goddess! True volunteers versus
regulars.

As sturdy Republicans, we lingered long upon
this spot. Will you lay " violent hands upon the
Lord's anointed?" " I'll anoint ye!" says he, and
then, I take it, was settled for the future the " divine
right of kings" theory ; for since then these curious
appendages of a free state have been kept for show,

and we hear nothing any more of the "divinity which doth hedge a king." Some one of the party remarked that we had not seen a statue or even a picture of England's great Protector. I told them a wise man once said that the reason Cromwell's statue was not put among those of the other rulers of England at Westminster was because he would dwarf them. But his day is coming. We shall have him there in his proper place by and by, and how small hereditary rulers will seem beside him!

Booth may not be great in anything, as some think, but I do not know his equal in "Richelieu;" and in one scene in particular he has always seemed to me at his very best. The king sits with his new minister Baradas in attendance at his side. Richelieu reclines upon a sofa exhausted while his secretaries "deliver up the papers of a realm." A secretary is on his knee presenting papers. He says:

"The affairs of England, Sire, most urgent. Charles
The First has lost a battle that decides
One half his realm—craves moneys, Sire, and succor.
   KING. He shall have both. Eh, Baradas?
   BARADAS.   Yes, Sire.
   RICHELIEU. (*Feebly, but with great distinctness.*) My liege—
Forgive me—Charles's cause is lost. A man,
Named Cromwell, risen—*a great man*—"

That is enough, a great man *settles* things; a small one nibbles away at petty reforms, although he knows nothing is settled thereby, and that the question is only pushed ahead for the time to break out again directly. English politicians are mostly nibblers, though Gladstone can take a good bite when put to it.

Our route lay through Warwick and Leamington. The view of the castle from the bridge is, I believe, the best of its kind in England. "From turret to foundation stone" it is all perfect. The very entrance tells of the good old days. As we pass beneath the archway, over the drawbridge, and under the portcullis, it all comes back to us.

> "Up drawbridge, grooms! What, Warder, ho!
> Let the portcullis fall!
> To pass there was such scanty room
> The bars descending razed his plume."

Warwick, the kingmaker! This was his castle. His quarrel with the king was one of our most taking recitations. I was considered great in this.

> "Know this, the man who injured Warwick
> Never passed uninjured yet."

He found that out, did he not, my lord of the ragged staff!

The view from the great hall looking on the river below is fixed in my mind. Don't miss it; and surely he who will climb to the top of Guy's Tower will have cause for thankfulness for many a year thereafter. You get a look at more of England there than is generally possible. I sympathize with Ruskin in his rage at the attempt to raise funds by subscription to mend the ravages of a recent fire in the castle. A Warwick in the rôle of a Belisarius begging for an obolus! If the kingmaker could look upon this! But historical names are now often trailed in the dust in England.

Driving through Leamington we reached Kenilworth Castle for luncheon, to which we had looked forward for several days. Alas! the keeper informed us that no pic-nic parties are admitted since the grounds have been put into such excellent order by the kind Earl Clarendon (for which thanks, good earl). But he was a man of some discrimination, this custodian of the ruins, and when he saw our four-in-hand and learned who we were—Americans! Brighton to Inverness!—he made us an exception to the rule, of which I trust his lordship will approve, if he ever hears. We had one of our happiest luncheons beneath the walls under a large hawthorn tree, which we decided was the very place where the enraged Queen Bess discovered dear Amy Robsart on that memorable night.

A thousand memories cluster round this ruin; but what should we have known of it had not the great magician touched with his wand this dead mass of stone and lime and conferred immortality upon the actors and their revels. To *do* things is not one half the battle in this world. Carlyle is all wrong about this. To be able to tell the world what you have done, that is the greater accomplishment! Cæsar is the greatest man of the sword because he was in his day the greatest man of the pen. Had he known how to fight only, tradition would have handed down his name for a few generations with a tolerably correct account of his achievements; but now every school-boy fights over again his battles and surmounts the difficulties he surmounted, and so his fame goes on increasing forever.

What a man says too often outlives what he does, even when he does great things. General Grant's fame is not to rest upon the fact that he was successful in killing his fellow-citizens in a civil war, all traces of which America wishes to obliterate, but upon the words he said now and then. His " Push things!" will influence Americans when Vicksburg shall be forgotten. " I propose to fight it out on this line" will be part of the language when few will remember when it was spoken ; and " Let us have peace" is Grant's most lasting monument. Truly, both the pen and the tongue are mightier than the sword !

This day was very warm, even for Americans, and after luncheon we became a lazy, sleepy party. I have a distinct recollection of an upward and then a downward movement which awoke me suddenly. One after another of the party, caught asleep on a rug, was treated to a tossing amid screams of laughter. We were all very drowsy, but a fresh breeze arose as the sun declined, and remounting the coach late in the afternoon we had a charming drive to Stratford-on-Avon.

STRATFORD-ON-AVON, June 23.

Our resting-place was the Red Horse Inn, of which Washington Irving has written so delightfully. One can hardly say that he comes into Shakespeare's country, for one is always there, so deeply and widely has his influence reached. We live in his land always ; but, as we approached the quiet little village where he appeared on earth, we could not help speculating upon the causes which produced the prodigy. One almost expects nature herself to present a different aspect to enable us to account in some measure for the apparition of a being so far beyond all others ; but it is not so—we see only the quiet beauty which characterizes almost every part of England. His sweet sonnets seem the natural outbirth of the land. Where met he the genius of tragedy, think you! Surely not on the cultivated banks of the gentle Avon, where all is so tame. But as Shakespeare resembled other burghers of Stratford so much, not showing upon the surface that he was that

> "largest son of time
> Who wandering sang to a listening world,"

our search for external conditions as to his environment need not be continued. Ordinary laws are inapplicable—he was a law unto himself. How or why Shakespeare was Shakespeare will be settled when there shall be few problems of the race left to settle. It is well that he lies on the banks of the Avon, for that requires us to make a special visit to his shrine to worship him. His mighty shade alone fills the mind. True monotheists are we all who make the pilgrimage to Stratford. I have been there often, but I am always awed into silence as I approach the church; and when I stand beside the ashes of Shakespeare I cannot repress stern, gloomy thoughts, and ask why so potent a force is now but a little dust. The inexplicable waste of nature, a million born that one may live, seems nothing compared to this—the brain of a god doing its work one day and food for worms the next! No wonder, George Eliot, that this was ever the weight that lay upon your heart and troubled you so!

A cheery voice behind me. "What is the matter? Are you ill? You look as if you hadn't a friend in the world!" Thanks, gentle remembrancer. This is no time for the chief to forget himself. We are not out for lessons or for moralizing. Things are and shall be "altogether lovely." One must often laugh if one would not cry.

Here is a funny conceit. A worthy draper in the town has recently put an upright stone at the head of his wife's grave, with an inscription setting forth the dates of her birth and death, and beneath it the following verse :

"For the Lord has done great things for us, whereof we are exceeding glad."

The wretch ! One of the wives of our party declared that she could not like a man who could think at such a crisis of such a verse, no matter how he meant it. She was confident that he was one of those terribly-resigned kind of men who will find that the Lord has done great things for him in the shape of a second helpmeet within two years.

This led to a search for other inscriptions. Here is one which struck our fancy :

"Under these ashes lies one close confined,
Who was to all both affable and kind ;
A neighbor good, extensive to ye poor,
Her soul we hope's at rest forevermore."

This was discussed and considered to go rather too far. Good Swedenborgians still dispute about the body's rising again, and make a great point of that, as showing their superior wisdom ; but this good friend seems to bespeak rest forever for the soul. One of us spoke of having lately seen a very remarkable collection of passages from Scripture

which seemed to permit the hope that all for whom
a kind father has nothing better in store than perpetual torture will kindly be permitted to rest. One
of the passages in question was: "For the wicked
shall *perish* everlastingly." The question was re-
mitted to the theologians of our party, with instruc-
tions to give it prayerful consideration and report.

If there be scriptural warrant for the belief, I
wish to embrace it at once. Meanwhile I am not
going to be sure that any poor miserable sinner is
to be disturbed when after "life's fitful fever he
sleeps well" on the tender, forgiving bosom of mother
earth, unless he can be *finally* fitted for as good or
a better life than this. Therefore, good Emma and
Ella and the rest who are staunch dogmatists, be
very careful how you report, for it is a fearful thing
to charge our Creator unjustly with decreeing ever-
lasting torture even to the worst offender into whom
he has breathed the breath of life. Refrain, if possible,

"Under this conjuration speak;
For we will hear, note, and believe in heart
That what you speak is in your conscience washed
As pure as sin with baptism."

I have not yet been favored with the report asked
for, and therefore the question rests.

We had one of the loveliest mornings imaginable
for leaving Stratford. Many had assembled to see
the start, and our horn sounded several parting
blasts as we crossed the bridge and rode out of the
town. Our destination was Coventry, twenty-two
miles away, and the route lay through Charlecote
Park and Hampton Lucy. This was one of the most

perfect of all our days. The deer in hundreds gazed on us as we passed. There were some noble stags in the herd, the finest we had seen in England, and Charlecote House was the best specimen of an Elizabethan mansion. It was for poaching in this very park that Shakespeare was fined by Squire Lucy (Justice Shallow). He probably wanted a taste of venison which was denied him. The descendant of that squire, my gentle Shakespeare, would give you the entire herd for another speech to "the poor sequestered stag," which you could dash off—no, you never dashed off anything; create? no; evolved? that's nearer it; *distilled*—there we have it—distilled as the pearls of dew are distilled by nature's sweet influences unknown to man. He would exchange Charlecote estate, man, for another Hamlet or Macbeth, or Lear or Othello, and the world would buy it from him for double the cost of all his broad acres, and esteem itself indebted to him forever. The really precious things of this world are its books.

The drive from Warwick to Leamington is famous, but not comparable to that between Leamington and Coventry. Nowhere else can be found such an avenue of stately trees; for many miles a strip about two hundred feet wide on both sides of the road is wooded. In passing through this plantation many a time did we bless the good, kind, thoughtful soul who generations ago laid posterity under so great an obligation. Dead and gone, his name known to the local antiquary and appreciated by a few of the district, but never heard of beyond it. "So shines a good deed in a naughty world." Receive the warm thanks and God bless you of pilgrims from a land, now containing the majority of the English-speaking races, which was not even born when you planted these stately trees. Americans come to bless your memory; for what says Sujata:

> "For holy books teach when a man shall plant
> Trees for the travellers' shade, and dig a well
> For the folks' comfort, and beget a son,
> It shall be good for such after their death."

Who shall doubt that it is well with the dear, kind soul who planted the thousand trees which delighted us this day, nodding their graceful boughs in genial welcome to the strangers and forming a triumphal arch in their honor!

COVENTRY, June 24.

Coventry in these days has a greater than Godiva. George Eliot stands alone among women; no second near that throne. We visited the little school-room where she learnt her first lessons; but more than that, the Mayor, who kindly conducted us through the city, introduced us to a man who had been her teacher. "I knew the strange little thing well," he said. A proud privilege indeed! I would have given much to know George Eliot, for many reasons. I heard with something akin to fellowship that she longed to be at every symphony, oratorio, or concert of classical music, and rarely was that strong, brooding face missed at such feasts. Indeed it was through attending one of these that she caught the cold which terminated fatally. Music was a passion with her, as she found in it calm and peace for the troubled soul tossed and tried by the sad, sad things of life. I understand this. A friend told me that a lady friend of hers, who was staying at the hotel in Florence where George Eliot was, made her acquaintance casually without knowing her name. Something, she knew not what, attracted her to her, and after a few days she began sending flowers to the strange woman. Completely fascinated, she went almost daily for hours to sit with her. This continued for many days, the lady using the utmost freedom, and not without feeling that the attention was pleasing to the queer, plain, and unpretending Englishwoman. One day she discovered by chance who her companion really was. Never before, as she said, had she felt such mortification. She went timidly to George Eliot's room and took her hand in hers, but shrank back unable to speak, while the tears rolled down her cheeks. "What is wrong?" was asked, and then the explanation came. "I didn't know who you were. I never suspected *it was you!*" Then came George Eliot's turn to be embarrassed. "You did not know I was George Eliot, but you were drawn to plain me all for my own self, a woman? I am so happy." She kissed the American lady tenderly, and the true friendship thus formed knew no end, but ripened to the close.

The finest thing not in her works that I know this genius to have said is this: Standing one day leaning upon the mantel she remarked: "I can imagine the coming of a day when the effort to relieve human beings in distress will be as involuntary upon the part of the beholder as to clasp this mantel would be this moment on my part were I about to fall." There's an ideal for you! Christ might have said that.

One thing more about our heroine, and a grand thing, said by Colonel Ingersoll. "In the court of her own conscience she sat pure as light, stainless as a star." I believe that, my dear Colonel. Why can you not give the world such gems as you are capable of, and let us alone about future things, concerning which you know no more than the new-born babe?

There is a good guide-book for Coventry, and there's much to tell about that city. It was once the ecclesiastical centre of England. Parliaments have sat there and great things have been done in Coventry. Many curious and valuable papers are seen in the hall. There is the order of Queen Elizabeth to her truly and well-beloved Mayor of Coventry, directing him to assist Earls Huntingdon and Shrewsbury in good charge of Mary Queen of Scots. There is a mace given by Cromwell to the corporation. You see that ruler of men could bestow maces as well as order his troopers to "take away that bauble" when the commonwealth required nursing. These and many more rare treasures are kept in an old building which is not fire-proof—a clear tempting of Providence. If I ever become so great a man as a councillor of Coventry, my maiden speech shall be upon the enormity of this offence. A councillor who carried a vote for a fire-proof building should some day reach the mayorship. This is a hint to our friends there.

The land question still troubles England, but even in Elizabeth's time it was thought not unconstitutional to fix rents arbitrarily. Here lies an edict of Her Majesty good Queen Bess, fixing the rates for pasturage on the commons near Coventry: "For one cow per week, one penny; for one horse, twopence." Our agriculturists should take this for a basis, a Queen Elizabeth valuation! I suppose some expert or other could figure the "fair rent" for anything, if given this basis to start upon.

The churches are very fine, the stained-glass windows excelling in some respects any we have seen, the amount of it is so much greater. The entire end of one of the cathedral churches is filled by three immense windows reaching from floor to roof, the effect of which is very grand. The choir of this church is not in line with the other portion of the building. In reply to my inquiry why this was so, the guide boldly assured us, with a look of surprise at our ignorance, that all cathedrals are so constructed, and that the crooked choir symbolizes the head of Christ, which is always represented leaning to one side of the cross. The idea made me shiver; I felt as if I should never be able to walk up the aisle of a cathedral again without an unpleasant sensation. Thanks to a clear-headed, thorough-going young lady, who "just didn't believe it," we soon got at the truth about cathedrals, for she proved that they are everywhere built on straight lines. This guide fitly illustrates the danger of good men staying at home in their little island. His cathedral is crooked, and therefore all others are or should be so. Very English this, very. There are many things still crooked in the dear old tight little isle which other lands have straightened out long ago, or rather never built crooked. Hurry up, you leader of nations in generations past! It's not your rôle in the world to lag behind ; at least it has not been till lately, when others have "bettered your instruction." Come along, England, you are not done for ; only stir yourself, and the lead is still yours. The guide was a theological student, and therefore could not be expected to have much general knowledge, but he surely should have known something about cathedrals.

It rained at Coventry during breakfast, and friend Graham ventured to suggest that perhaps some of the ladies might prefer going by rail to Birmingham and join the coach there at luncheon ; but

> "He did not know the stuff
> Of our gallent crew, so tough,
> On board the Charioteer O."

He was "morally sat upon," as Lucy says. Not a lady but indignantly repelled the suggestion. Even Mrs. Graham, a bride, and naturally somewhat in awe of her husband yet, went so far as to say "Tom is queer this morning."

Waterproofs and umbrellas to the front, we sallied forth from the courtyard of the Queen's in a drenching down-pour.

> "But what care we how wet we be,
> By the coach we'll live or die."

That was the sentiment which animated our breasts. For my part I was very favorably situated, and I held my umbrella very low to shield my fair charge the better. Of course I greatly enjoyed the first few miles under such conditions. My young lady broke into song, and I thought I caught the sense of the words, which I fondly imagined was something like this:

> "For if you are under an umbrella
> With a very handsome fellow,
> It cannot matter much what the weather may be."

I asked if I had caught the words correctly, but she archly insinuated there was something in the second line that wasn't quite correct. I think, though, she was only in fun; the words were quite right, only her eyes seemed to wander in the direction of young Bantock.

None of the ladies would go inside, so Joe had the compartment all to himself, and no doubt smiled at the good joke as we bowled along. Joe was dry inside, and Perry, though outside, was just the same ere we found an inn. This recalled the story of the coachman and the Oxford Don, when the latter expressed his sympathy at the condition of the former; so sorry he was so wet. "Wouldn't mind being so wet, your honor, if I weren't so *dry*." But I think Robert Pitcairn's story almost as good as that. A Don tried to explain to the coachman the operation of the telegraph as they drove along. "They take a glass about the size of an ordinary tumbler, and this they fill with a liquid resembling—ah—like—ah—" "Anything like beer, your honor, for instance?" If Jehu didn't get his complimentary glass at the next halt, that Don was a muff.

The rain ceased, as usual, before we had gone far, and we had a clear dry run until luncheon. We see the Black Country now, rows of little dingy houses beyond, with tall smoky chimneys vomiting smoke, mills and factories at every turn, coal pits and rolling mills and blast furnaces, the very bottomless pit itself; and such dirty, careworn children, hard-driven men, and squalid women. To think of the green lanes, the larks, the Arcadia we have just left. How can people be got to live such terrible lives as they seem condemned to here? Why do they not all run away to the green fields just beyond? Pretty rural Coventry suburbs in the morning and Birmingham at noon; the lights and shadows of human existence can rarely be brought into sharper contrast. If

"Better fifty years of Europe than a cycle of Cathay,"

surely better a month in Leamington than life's span in the Black Country! But do not let us forget that it is just Pittsburgh over again; nay, not even quite so bad, for that city bears the palm for dirt against the world. The fact is, however, that life in such places seems attractive to those born to rural life, and large smoky cities drain the country; but surely this may be safely attributed to necessity. With freedom to choose, one would think the rush would be the other way. The working classes in England do not work so hard or so unceasingly as do their fellows in America. They have ten holidays to the American's one. Neither does their climate entail such a strain upon men as ours does.

I remember after Vandy and I had gone round the world and were walking Pittsburgh streets, we decided that the Americans were the saddest-looking race we had seen. Life is so terribly earnest here. Ambition spurs us all on, from him who handles the spade to him who employs thousands. We know no rest. It is different in the older lands—men rest oftener and enjoy more of what life has to give. The young Republic has some things to teach the parent land, but the elder has an important lesson to teach the younger in this respect. In this world we must learn not to lay up our treasures, but to enjoy them day by day as we travel the path we never return to. If we fail in this we shall find when we do come to the days of leisure that we have lost the taste for and the capacity to enjoy them. There are so many unfortunates cursed with plenty to retire upon, but with nothing to retire to! Sound wisdom that school-boy displayed who did not "believe in putting away for to-morrow the cake he could eat to-day." It might not be fresh on the morrow, or the cat might steal it. The cat steals many a choice bit from Americans intended for the morrow. Among the saddest of all spectacles to me is that of an elderly man occupying his last years grasping for more dollars. "The richest man in America sailing suddenly for Europe to escape business cares," said a wise Scotch gentleman to me, one morning, as he glanced over the *Times* at breakfast. Make a note of that, my enterprising friends.

We spent the afternoon in Birmingham, and enjoyed a great treat in the Town Hall, in which there is one of the best organs of the world. It is played every Saturday by an eminent musician, admission free. This is one of the little—no, one of the great—things done for the masses in many cities in England, the afternoon of Saturday being kept as a holiday everywhere.

Here is the programme for Saturday, June 25th:

Town Hall Organ Recital.
BY MR. STIMPSON.
FROM 3 TILL 4 O'CLOCK.

Programme for June 25, 1881:

1. *Overture to A Midsummer Night's Dream,*   *Mendelssohn.*
   (It will only be necessary to state this descriptive Overture was written in Berlin, August 6, 1826. Shakespere and Mendelssohn must have been kindred spirits, for surely no more poetic inspiration ever came from the pen of any musical composer than the Overture of the great German master.)

2. *Romanza,*   - - - - - - *Haydn.*
   (This charming Movement is taken from the Symphony which Haydn wrote in 1786, for Paris, entitled "La Reine de France," and has been arranged for the organ by Mr. Best, of Liverpool.)

3. *Offertoire, in F major,* - - - *Batiste.*
   (All the works of the French masters, Wely, Batiste, Guilmant, and Saint-Saens, if not severely classical, have a certain grace and charm which make them acceptable to even the most prejudiced admirers of the ancient masters; and this Offertoire of Batiste is one of the most popular of his compositions.)

4. *Fugue in G minor,* - - - - *J. S. Bach.*
   (It may interest connoisseurs to know this grand Fugue was selected by the Umpires for the trial of skill when the present Organist of the Town Hall was elected.)

5. *Jaglied (Hunting Song),* - - - *Schumann.*

6. *Selection from the Opera "Martha,"* - - *Flotow.*
   (The Opera from which this selection is taken was written in Vienna, in 1847, and, in conjunction with "Stradella," at once stamped the name of the author as one of the most popular of the dramatic composers of the present day.)

7. *Dead March in Saul,* - - - - *Handel.*

In Memoriam, Sir Josiah Mason.

Price One Halfpenny.

The next Free Organ Recital will be given on July 2d,
AT THREE O'CLOCK.

A HISTORY OF THE TOWN HALL ORGAN (A NEW EDITION, REVISED AND ENLARGED), BY MR. STIMPSON,

Is now ready, and may be had in the Town Hall, and at the Midland Educational Co.'s Warehouse, New Street.

NOTICE.—A box will be placed at each door to receive contributions, to defray the expenses of these Recitals.

Miss Johns said she had never before heard an organ so grandly played, and she knows. The management of the left hand in the fugue she declared wonderful. It is best to give the best for the masses, even in music, the highest of our gifts. John Bright has made most of his speeches in this hall, but it is no longer large enough for the Liberal demonstrations, and a much larger structure has been erected.

The eleven miles between Birmingham and Wolverhampton are nothing but one vast iron-working, coal-mining establishment. There is scarcely a blade of grass of any kind to be seen, and not one real clean pure blade did we observe during the journey. It was Saturday afternoon and the mills were all idle, and the operatives thronged the villages through which we drove. O mills and furnaces and coal-pits and all the rest of you, you may be necessary, but you are no bonnie! Pittsburghers though many of us were, inured to smoke and dirt, we felt the change very deeply from the hedgerows, the green pastures, the wild flowers and pretty clean cottages, and voted the district "horrid." Wolverhampton's steeples soon came into sight, and we who had been there and could conjure up dear, honest, kindly faces waiting to welcome us with warm hearts, were quite restored to our usual spirits, notwithstanding dirt and squalor. The sun of a warm welcome from friends gives many clouds a silver lining, and it did make the black country brighter. The coach and horses, and Joe and Perry, not to mention our generalissimo Graham, belong to Wolverhampton, as you know, and our arrival had been looked for by many. The crowd was quite dense in the principal street as we drove through. One delegation after another was left at friends' houses, the Charioteers having been billeted upon the connection; and here for the first time we were to enjoy a respite.

WOLVERHAMPTON, June 25-30.

We were honored by an entertainment at his Honor the Mayor's. As usual on fine days in England, the attractions of the mansion (and they are not small in this case) gave place to open-air enjoyments on the lawn—the game, the race, the stroll, and all the rest of the sports which charm us in this climate. The race across the lawn was far better fun than the Derby, but our gentlemen must go into strict training before they challenge those English girls again. It is some consolation that Iroquois has since vindicated the glory of the Republic.

We coached one day about fourteen miles to Apley House, and had a joyous picnic day with our friends Mr. and Mrs. Sing, of Newton. The party numbered seventy odd, great and small. That day the Charioteers agreed should be marked as a red-letter day in their annals, for surely never was a day's excursion productive of more enjoyment to all of us. There are few, if any, prettier views in England than that from the terrace at Apley House. The Vale of Severn deserves its reputation. We had a trip on the river for several miles from Bridgenorth to the grounds as part of the day's pleasure.

How very small England's great rivers are! I remember how deeply hurt Mr. Franks was when his Yankee nephew (H. P. Jr., Our Pard) visited him for the first time, and was shown the river by his uncle, who loved it. "Call this a river?" exclaimed he, "why, it's only a creek! I could almost jump across it there"—but H. P. was young then, and would not have hesitated to "speak disrespectfully of the equator" upon occasion. I won the good man's heart at once by saying that small though it was in size (and what has either he or I to boast of in that line, I wonder), little Severn filled a larger space in the world's destiny and the world's thoughts than twenty mighty streams. Listen :

> "Three times they breathed and three times did they drink,
> Upon agreement of swift Severn's flood,
> Who then, affrighted with their bloody looks,
> Ran fearfully among the trembling reeds
> And hid his crisp head in the hollow bank,
> Blood-stained with these violent combatants."

Why, you have not a river like that in all America. H. P. was judiciously silent. But I do not think he was ever quite forgiven. These Americans have always such big ideas.

The free library at Wolverhampton interested me. I do not know where better proof of the advantages of such an institution is to be found. It was started upon a small scale, about fifteen thousand dollars being expended; now some forty thousand dollars have been spent upon the building. Last year eighty-six thousand books were issued. I counted at noon, June 30th, sixty-three persons in the reading-room, and at another time nearly two hundred readers. On Saturdays, between two and ten P.M., the number averages fully a thousand. In addition to the circulating library, there are a reference library, a museum, and large reading-rooms. Several courses of lectures are connected with the institution, with teachers for the various branches. One teacher, a Mr. Williams, has " passed " scholars in the science and art department every year, and one year every one of his scholars passed the Kensington examination. A working plumber who attended these classes gained prizes for chemistry and electricity, and is now secretary of the water-works at Chepstow. We may hear more of that climber yet. Plenty of room at the top! No sectarian papers are subscribed for, but all reputable publications are received if sent. In this way all sects are represented by their best, if the members see fit to contribute them. This is the true plan. " Error may be tolerated if truth be free to combat it. Let truth and error grapple." The city levies one penny per pound upon the rates, as authorized by the libraries act. This nets about four thousand dollars per annum. Just see what powerful agencies for the improvement of the people can be set on foot for a trifling sum.

Wolverhampton is a go-ahead city (I note a strong Scotch element there). A fine park has recently been acquired and laid out with taste. This shows that the physical well-being of the people is not lost sight of. The administration of our friend ex-Mayor Dickinson is to be credited with this invaluable acquisition. Mr. Dickinson took the most prominent part in the matter, and having succeeded he can consider the park his own estate. It is not in any sense taken away from him, nor one of its charms lessened because his fellow-citizens share its blessings. Indeed as I strolled through it with him I thought the real sense of ownership must be sweeter from the thousands of his fellows whom we saw rejoicing within it than if he were indeed the lordly owner in fee and rented it for revenue. This whole subject of meum and tuum needs reconsideration. If Burns, when he held his plough in joy upon the mountain-side and saw what he saw, felt what he felt, was not more truly the real possessor of the land than the reputed nominal landlord, then I do not grasp the subject. There are woeful blunders made as to the ownership of things. Who owns the treasures of the Sunderland or Hamilton libraries? and who will shed the tears over their dispersion think you, chief mourner by virtue of deepest loss, the titled dis-graces, in whose names they stand, or the learned librarian whose days have been spent in holy companionship with them? It is he who has made them his own, drawn them from their miserable owners into his heart. I tell you a man cannot be the real owner of a library or a picture gallery without a title from a much higher tribunal than the law. Nor a horse either, for that matter. Who owns your favorite horse? Test it! I say the groom does. Call Habeeb or Roderick. So slow their response! I won't admit they don't know and like me too. John knows my weakness and stands, out of sight and lets me succeed slowly with them; but after that, see at one word from him how they prick up their ears and neigh, dance in their boxes, push their grand heads under his arm, and say as plainly as can be, "This is our man." I'm only a sleeping partner with John in them after all. It's the same all through; go to your dogs, or out to your flocks, and see every sheep, and even the little lambs, the cows with their kind, glowering eyes, the chickens, and every living thing run from you to throng round the hand that feeds them. There is no real purchase in money, you must win friendship and ownership in the lower range of life with kindness, companionship, love; the coin of the realm is not legal tender with Trust, or Habeeb, or Brownie, nor with any of the tribe.

We can tell you nothing of the hotels of Wolverhampton, but the fourteen of us can highly recommend certain quarters where it was our rare privilege to be honored guests. Whether the English eat and drink more than the Americans may be a debatable question, but they certainly do so oftener. The young ladies quartered at Newbridge reported this the only bar to perfect happiness; they never wanted to leave the garden for meals nor to remain so long at table. As Miss Jeannie reported, they just sound a gong and *spring* luncheons and teas and suppers on you. The supper is an English institution, even more sacred than the throne, and destined to outlive it. You cannot escape it, and to tell the truth, after a little you have no wish to do so. There is much enjoyment at supper, and in Scotland this is the toddy-time, and who would miss that hour of social glee!

Mention must be made of the private theatricals at Merridale and of the amateur concert at Clifton House, both highly creditable to the talented performers and productive of great pleasure to the guests. I find a programme of the latter and incorporate it as part of the record:

Clifton House, Wolverhampton,

JUNE 29TH, 1881.

☙ Programme ✥ of ✥ Music ☙

PIANOFORTE DUET	"Oberon" Misses A. J. and A. C. BANTOCK.	René Favayer
SONG	"Twenty-one" Miss SUSIE DICKINSON.	Molloy
SONG	"The Raft" Mr. BANTOCK PIERPOINT.	Pinsuti
LADIES' TRIO	"O Skylark, for thy wing" Misses BANTOCK and DICKINSON.	Smart
SONG	"A Summer Shower" Miss DICKINSON.	Marzials
SONG	"The Better Land" Miss M. BANTOCK.	Cowen
SONG	"The Lost Chord" Miss PIERPOINT.	Sullivan
PIANOFORTE SOLO	"La Cascade" Miss ALICE DICKINSON.	Pauer
SONG	"Let me dream again" Miss REID.	Sullivan
SONG	"The Diver" Mr. ARTHUR BANTOCK.	Loder
SONG	"My Nannie's awa'" Miss JEANNIE JOHNS.	——
DUET	"When the Wind blows in from the Sea" Miss M. BANTOCK and Mr. BANTOCK PIERPOINT.	Smart
SONG	"For ever and for ever" Miss A. J. BANTOCK.	Paolo Tosti
SONG	"The Boatswain's Story" Mr. BANTOCK PIERPOINT.	Molloy

GOD SAVE THE QUEEN.

A great many fine compliments have been paid to performers in this world, but do you remember one much better than this? Our Miss Jeannie sang "My Nannie's awa'," my favorite among twenty favorites; and she did sing it that night to perfection. We were all proud of our prima donna. When she returned to her seat next to Maggie, there was whispered in her ear: "Oh, Jeannie, the lump's in my throat yet!" All the hundred warm expressions bestowed upon her did not weigh as much as that little gem of a tribute. When you raise the lump in the throat by a song you are upon the right key and have the proper style, even if your teacher has been no other than your own heart, the most important teacher of all.

After the theatricals at Merridale came the feast. The supper-table comes before me, and the speeches. The orator of the Wolverhampton connection is ex-Mayor Bantock. He speaks well, and never did he appear to greater advantage than on that evening. It's a sight "gude for sair een" to see a good-natured, kindly English gentleman presiding at the festive board, surrounded by his children and his children's children, and the family connections to the number of seventy odd. They are indeed a kindly people, but oh dear! those who have never been out of their little island, even the most liberal of them, have such queer, restricted notions about the rest of mankind! This, however, is only natural; travel is in one sense the only possible educator. The best speech of the evening upon our side was made by Mr. Phipps, who said he felt that after he had forgotten all else about this visit, the smiling faces of the pretty, rosy-cheeked English young ladies he had been admiring ever since he came to Wolverhampton, and never more ardently than this evening, would still haunt his thoughts; and then, with more emphasis, he closed with these memorable words: "And I tell you, if ever young men ask me where they can find the nicest, sweetest, prettiest, and best young ladies for wives, they won't have to ask twice." (Correct! shake, Pard!)

We were fortunate in seeing the statue to Mr. Villiers unveiled. Earl Granville spoke with rare grace and ease, his style being so far beyond that of the other speakers that they suffered by comparison. The sledge-hammer style of oratory is done. Let ambitious youngsters make a note of that, and no longer strut and bellow, and tear a passion all to tatters, to very rags. Shakespeare understood it:

"In the very tempest and I may say whirlwind of your passion,
You must beget a temperance to give it utterance."

The effort now making throughout Great Britain to provide coffee-houses as substitutes for the numerous gin palaces has not been neglected in Wolverhampton. The Coffee House Company which operates in the city and neighborhood has now fourteen houses in successful operation, and, much to my astonishment and gratification, I learned that seven and a half per cent dividends were declared and about an equal amount of profit reserved for contingencies. In Birmingham there are twenty houses, and cash dividends of ten per cent per annum have been made. If they can be generally made to pay even half as well, a grand advance has been made in the war against intemperance. I visited one of the houses with Mr. Dickinson, who, I rejoice to say, is Chairman of the Company, and in this great office does more for the cause than a thousand loud-mouthed orators who only denounce the evil about which we are all agreed, but have no plan to suggest for overcoming it. It is so easy to denounce and tear down; but try to build up once and see what slow, discouraging labor is involved.

The prices in these coffee-houses are very low: one large cup of good tea, coffee, or cocoa, at the counter, 1d (2 cents); one sandwich, 1d (2 cents). If taken upstairs in a room at a table, one half more.

There is a reading-room with newspapers free, bagatelle-table, and comfortable sitting-rooms; also a ladies' room and a lavatory, and cigars, tobacco, and all non-alcoholic drinks are provided. Men go there at night to read and to play games. The company has been operating for three years, and the business increases steadily. We saw similar houses in most of the towns we passed, and wished them God-speed.

A chairman of a company like this has it in his power to do more good for the masses, who are the people of England, than if he occupied his time as member of Parliament; but the English exalt politics unduly and waste the lives of their best men disputing over problems which the more advanced Republicans have settled long ago and cleared out of their way. They will learn better by and by. We must not be impatient. They are a slow race and prone to makeshifts politically.

"Nae man can tether time nor tide,
 The hour approaches, Tam must [let us] ride."

Our six days at Wolverhampton had passed rapidly away in one continual round of social pleasures, and now we were off again to fresh fields and pastures new. The horn sounds. We call the roll once more. Mr. Beck Senior had left us at Windsor, but the Junior Beck he sent us fitly represented the family. If he couldn't tell as many funny stories nor quote as much poetry as his sire, the young Cambridge wrangler could sing college songs and give our young ladies many glimpses of young England. He was a great favorite was Theodore (young Obadiah).

Miss Beck and he left us at Banbury, much to our regret, but London engagements were imperative. Mr. and Mrs. King arrived. If ever a couple received a warmer welcome I never saw or heard of it. It seemed as if we had been separated for years, and how often during our journey had one or another of the party regretted that Aggie and Aaleck were missing all this.

It was upon the ocean that Ben and Davie conceived the idea that a run to Paris would be advisable. Leave of absence for two weeks was accordingly granted to four—Mr. and Mrs. McCargo, Miss Johns, and Mr. Vandevort.

We bade them good-bye at Wolverhampton, Thursday, June 30th, and saw them fairly off, not without tears upon both sides from the weaker sex. These partings are miserable things always. Their places were taken by Miss Jeannie Reid (a Dunfermline bairn), Miss Amelia Bantock, and Mr. Dickinson. Next morning we gathered the clans at Mr. Graham's, calling at Mr. Ben Bantock's and at Mr. Thomas's for the contingent they had so kindly entertained ; thence to Mr. Dickinson's, and then to Merridale for the remainder and the final start.

It was a sight to see the party on the lawn there as we drove off, giving three hearty cheers for Wolverhampton. In special honor of the head of the clan there, the master of Merridale, we had just sung "For he is an Englishman." Yes, he is the Englishman all over. Mr. Graham, no longer in his official capacity, however, drove out with Mr. Wilson several miles and saw us fairly off. The parting was a sad one. How we were to get on without our late general manager was a source of anxiety, but Mr. McCandless soon proved that he was a worthy successor, and from that parting till our arrival in New York his laurels increased. Our route for many miles was still in the black country, but near Lichfield we reached once more the rural beauties of England. How thankful to get away once more from the dirt and smoke and bustle of manufactories.

The new members had not gone far before they exhibited in an aggravated form all the usual signs of the mania which had attacked and so seriously affected all who have ever mounted our coach. The older members derived great pleasure from seeing how completely the recent acquisitions were carried away. Their enthusiasm knew no bounds, and we drove into the Swan at Lichfield brimful of happiness. We had left Wolverhampton about noon, the stage for the day being a short one, only twenty miles.

LICHFIELD, July 1.

The cathedral deserves a visit, out of the way of travel as it is. Its three spires and its chapter house are the finest we have yet seen; and then Chantrey's sleeping children is worth travelling hundreds of miles to see. Never before has marble been made to express the childish sleep of innocence as this does.

It was strange that I should stumble upon a monument in the cathedral to Major Hodson, whose grave I had visited in India. He lies with Havelock in the pretty little English cemetery at Lucknow, poor fellow, and here his friends and neighbors away in quiet Lichfield have commemorated his valor.

There are in the cathedral seven very fine stained-glass windows which were found stowed away in a farm-house in Belgium, and purchased by an English gentleman for £200, and now they rank among the most valuable windows in the world. What a pity that the treasures wantonly destroyed during the Reformation had not found similar shelter, to be brought from their hiding-places once more to delight us.

We heard service Saturday morning, and mourned over the waste of exquisite music—twenty-six singers in the choir and only ten persons to listen in the vast cathedral, besides our party. It is much the same throughout England. In no case during week days did we ever see as many persons in the congregation as in the choir. Surely the impressive cathedrals of England are capable of being put to greater uses than this. It seems a sin to have such choirs and not conduct them in some way to reach and elevate greater numbers. In no building would an oratorio sound so well. Why should not these choirs be made the nucleus for a chorus in every district, and let us have music which would draw the masses within the sacred walls? But maybe this would be sacrilegious. The theological mind may see in the music suggested an unworthy intruder in domains sacred to dogma. Some day, however, my lord bishop and lazy crew, the cathedrals of England will not be yours alone to drone in, but become mighty centres of grand music, from which shall radiate elevating influences over entire districts, and the best minds of the nation, remembering how narrow and bigoted the church was when these structures were built, will change the poet's line and say :

"To what great uses have they come at last!"

The world moves and the church establishment must move with it, or—this is a splendid place to stop—there is as great virtue in your "or" as in your "if," sometimes. Here is the best description of service in an English cathedral :

"And love the high embowered roof,
With antic pillars massy proof,
And storied windows richly dight,
Casting a dim religious light :
There let the pealing organ blow,
To the full voic'd choir below,
In service high, and anthems clear,
As may with sweetness, through my ear,
Dissolve me into ecstasies,
And bring all heav'n before mine eyes."

The music at Lichfield does indeed draw you into regions beyond and intimates immortality, and we exclaim with friend Izaak Walton, " Lord, what music hast thou provided for the saints in heaven, when thou affordest bad men such music on earth !"

I remember that when in China I read that Confucius was noted for his intense passion for music. He said one day to his disciples that music not only elevates man while he is listening to it, but that to those who love it it is able to create distinct images which remain after the strains cease and keep the mind from base thoughts. Think of the sage knowing this when he had probably only the sing-song Chinese fiddle to console him ! I forget, he had the gongs, and a set of fine gongs of different tones make most suggestive music, as I have discovered.

The position of Lichfield Cathedral is peculiarly fine. Three sides of the square surrounding it are occupied by fine ecclesiastical buildings connected with the diocese, including the bishop's palace. A beautiful sheet of water lies upon the lower side, so that nothing incongruous meets the eye.

We obtained there a better idea of the magnitude of the church establishment and its to us seemingly criminal waste of riches than ever before. To think of all this power for good wasting itself upon a beggarly account of empty benches, the choir outnumbering the congregation !

We had ordered the coach to come and await us at the cathedral, but had not expected Perry to drive up to the very door. There the glittering equipage was, however, surrounded by groups of pretty, rosy children and many older people gazing respectfully.

We mounted and drove off, taking a last fond look of grand old Lichfield.

DOVEDALE, July 2-3.

Our objective point was Dovedale, thirty miles distant. When three miles out we stopped at Elmhurst Hall for Miss French, who had preceded us to pay a visit to Mr. and Mrs. Fox, who very kindly invited the party to dismount and lunch with them; but the thirty miles to be done would not permit us the pleasure. The next time we pass, however, good master and mistress of Elmhurst Hall, you shall certainly have the Charioteers within your hospitable walls, if you desire it, for such an inviting place we have rarely seen. Miss French remained with them over Sunday and joined us at Rowsley on Monday.

We were to lunch in Sudbury Park, the residence of Lord Vernon. This was the first grassy luncheon of the five new-comers, and we were all delighted to see their enjoyment of this most Arcadian feature of our coaching life. It proved to be one of our pleasantest luncheons, for there is no finer spot in England than Sudbury Park. Of course it is not the glen nor the wimpling burn of the Highlands, but for quiet England it is superb.

The site chosen was near a pretty brook. Before us was the old-fashioned brick Queen Anne mansion, and behind us in the park was a cricket ground, where a match between two neighboring clubs was being worthily contested. The scene was indeed idyllic. There was never more fun and laughter at any of our luncheons. Aaleck had to be repressed at last, for several of the members united in a complaint against him. Their sides ached, but that they did not mind so much; their anxiety was about their cheeks, which were seriously threatened with an explosion if they attempted to eat. To avoid such results it was voted that no one should make a joke nor even a remark. Silence was enjoined; but what did that amount to! The signs and grimaces were worse than speech. Force was no remedy. It took time to get the party toned down, but eventually the lunch was finished.

We strolled over and watched the cricketers. It all depends upon how you look at a thing. So many able-bodied perspiring men knocking about a little ball on a warm summer's day, that is one way; so many men relieved from anxious care and laying the foundation for long years of robust health by invigorating exercise in the open air, that is the other view of the question. The ancients did not count against our little span of life the days spent in the chase; neither need we charge those spent in cricket; and as for our sport, coaching, for every day so spent we decided that it and another might safely be credited. He was a very wise prime minister who said he had often found important duties for which he had not time; one duty, however, he had always *made* time for, his daily afternoon ride on horseback. Your always busy man accomplishes little; the great doer is he who has plenty of leisure. The man at the helm turns the wheel now and then, and so easily too, touching an electric bell; it's the stoker down below who is pitching into it with his coat off. And look at Captain McMicken promenading the deck in his uniform and a face like a full moon; quite at his ease and ready for a story. And there is Johnnie Watson, chief engineer, who rules over the throbbing heart of the ship: he is standing there prepared for a crack. Moral —Don't worry yourself over work, hold yourself in reserve, and sure as fate, " it will all come right in the wash."

Leaving the contestants, we walked down to the lake in front of the mansion, and with our usual good fortune we were just in time to see the twenty acres of ornamental water dragged for pike, which play such havoc with other fish. The water had been drained into a small pond, which seemed alive with bewildered fish. We sat and watched with quiet interest the men drawing the net. Hundreds were caught at every haul, from which the pike were taken. A tremendous eel gave the men a lively chase; three or four times it escaped, wriggled through their legs and hands one after the other, and made for the water. Had the gamekeeper not succeeded in pinning it to the ground with a pitchfork, the eel would have beaten the whole party.

Lord Vernon's park is rich in attractions. An old narrow picturesque arched bridge, which spans the pretty lake, has a statue of Adam at one end and Eve at the other. Over the former the ivy clusters so thickly as to make our great prototype a mass of living green; poor Eve has been less favored, for she is in a pitiable plight for a woman, with " nothing to wear."

But Eve was not used to kind treatment. Adam was by no means a modern model husband, and never gave Eve anything in excess except blame.

Here she is still, the Flora McFlimsy of my friend William Allen Butler (minus the flora as I have said); but let her be patient, her dress is sure to come, for kind nature in England abhors nakedness. She is ever at work clothing everything with her mantle of green.

> "Ever and ever bringing secrets forth,
> It sitteth in the green of forest glades
> Nursing strange seedlings at the cedar's root,
> Devising leaves, blooms, blades.
> This is its touch upon the blossomed rose,
> The fashion of its hand shaped lotus leaves;
> In dark soil and the silence of the seeds
> The robe of Spring it weaves."

We had rare enjoyment at the lake, and envied Lord Vernon his princely heritage. The old forester who once showed me over a noble estate in Scotland was quite right. I was enchanted with one of the views, and repeated,

> "Where is the coward who would not dare
> To fight for such a land!"

"Aye," said the old man, "aye, it's a grand country, *for the lairds.*" It will be a grander country some day when it is less "for the lairds" and more for the toiling masses; but may the destroying angel of progress look kindly upon such scenes of beauty as Sudbury Park. The extensive estate may be disentailed and cultivated by a thousand small owners in smiling homes, with educated children within them, and the land bring forth greater harvests touched by the magic wand of the sense of ownership, and yet the mansion and park remain intact and give to its possessor rarer pleasures than at present. I think one of the greatest drawbacks to life in Britain in grand style must be the contrast existing between the squire and the people about him. It is bad enough even in Chester Valley, where the average condition and education of the inhabitants are probably equal to any locality in the world, but in England it is far too marked for comfort, I should think.

While we were still lingering on the banks of the lake Perry's horn sounded from the main road to call us from the enchanting scene, and we were off for Dovedale through pretty Ashbourne.

Can any one picture a resting-place so full of peace and beauty as the old Izaak Walton Inn? (If you don't put in that k, Mr. Printer, there will be trouble.) We arrived there in the twilight, and some of us walked down the long hill and got our first sight of the Dove from the bridge at the foot across the stream.

I got the memorable verses near enough from memory to repeat them on the bridge. Let me put them down here, for in truth, simple as they are, who is going to predict the coming of the day when they will cease to be prized as one of the gems of literature?

"She dwelt among the untrodden ways,
   Beside the springs of Dove,
A maid whom there were none to praise,
   And very few to love.

"A violet by a mossy stone,
   Half hidden from the eye;
Fair as a star when only one
   Is shining in the sky.

"She lived unknown, and few could know
   When Lucy ceased to be;
But she is in her grave, and oh,
   The difference to me!"

But think of dear old Izaak and of his fishing excursions to this very spot. He actually stayed at our inn! He too is secure of his position as the author of a classic, for as long a time as we care to look forward to. Is it not strange that no one has ever imitated this man's unique style? "God leads us not to heaven by many nor by hard questions," says the fisherman, and he knew a thing or two. There is a flavor about him peculiarly his own, but especially rich when read in this old inn, sacred to his memory. I enjoyed him with a fresh relish during the few hours of Sunday which I could devote to him, for there is a good sermon in many a sentence of the "Complete Angler." Dear old boy, your place in my library and in my heart too is secure.

Ilam Hall, near the inn, is the great place, and there is a pretty little church within a stone's throw of it. We walked over on Sunday morning and saw the squire come into church with his family and take his seat among his people, for I take it most of the congregation were connected with the hall. The parson no doubt was the appointee of the squire, and we tried to estimate the importance of these two men in the district; their duties and influence—both great—for to a large extent the moral as well as the material well-being of a community in rural England depend upon the character of the hall and parsonage. The squire was Mr. Hanbury, M.P., who courteously invited our party to visit the hall after service, and to stroll as we pleased through his grounds. He had been in America, and knew our erratic genius and brother iron-master Abram S. Hewitt.

In the evening we received from him some fine photographs of the hall (a truly noble one), which we prize highly. The accompanying note was even more gratifying, for it said that he had been so warmly received in America that it was always a pleasure when opportunity offered to show Americans such attentions as might be in his power. It is ever thus, cold indifference between the two English-speaking branches is found only among the stay-at-homes. The man who knows from personal experience the leading characteristics of the people upon both sides of the ferry is invariably a warm and sincere friend. The two peoples have only to become acquainted to become enthusiastic over each other's rare qualities.

This is a sheep-grazing district, quite hilly, and the rainfall is much beyond the average; but the weather question troubles us little; the Charioteers carry sunshine within and without. Our afternoon walk was along the Dove, which we followed up the glen between the hills for several miles, finding new beauties at every turn. Mr. Hanbury has the stream on his estate reserved for five miles for his own fishing, but our landlord said he was very generous and always gave a gentleman a day's sport when properly applied for. We were offered free range by Mr. Hanbury, a privilege which Davie and I hold in reserve for a future day, that we may most successfully conjure the shade of our congenial brother of the angle; "for you are to note," saith he, "that we anglers all love one another." We at least all love Izaak Walton, "an excellent angler and now with God." Reading the ingenious defence of fishing by our author, "an honest man and a most excellent fly-fisher," is not waste time in these days of violent anti-vivisectionists, who have seen poor hares chased down for sport all their lives, and their Prince shoot pigeons from a trap without a protest, but who affect to feel pity for a cat sacrificed upon the holy altar of science. Miserable hypocrites, who swallow so large a camel and strain at so very small a gnat! It shows what demoralization is brought about in good people by rank and fashion; one rule for the Prince who disgraces himself by cruel sports, another for the medical student who exalts himself working for the good of his race.

But to quaint Izaak's defence; and first as to the fish themselves.

"Nay, the increase of these creatures that are bred and fed in water is not only more and more miraculous, but more advantageous to man, not only for the lengthening of his life, but for the preventing of sickness; for 'tis observed by the most learned physicians that the casting off of Lent and other fish days hath doubtless been the chief cause of those many putrid, shaking, intermitting agues into which this nation of ours is now more subject than those wiser countries which feed on herbs, salads, and plenty of fish. And it is fit to remember that Moses (Levit. 11:9; Deut. 14:9) appointed fish to be the chief diet for the best commonwealth that ever yet was; and it is observable not only that there are fish, as namely the whale, three times as big as the mighty elephant that is so fierce in battle, but that the mightiest feasts have been of fish."

Is not that capital? It calls to mind Josh Billings's answer to his correspondent who wrote saying that he had heard many times that a fish diet was most favorable for increase of brain power, but he had never been able to find out the best kind of fish for the purpose. Could he inform him? "In your case," replied Josh, "try a whale or two."

Here is Izaak's argument for the lawfulness of fishing:

"And for the lawfulness of fishing it may very well be maintained by our Saviour's bidding St. Peter cast his hook into the water and catch a fish for money to pay tribute to Cæsar. And it is observable that it was our Saviour's will that four fishermen should have a priority of nomination in the catalogue of his twelve disciples (Matt. 10 : 2, 4, 13), as namely : St. Peter, St. Andrew, St. James, and St. John, and then the rest in their order. And it is yet more observable that when our blessed Saviour went up into the mount when he left the rest of his disciples and chose only three to bear him company at his transfiguration that those three were all fishermen ; and it is to be believed that all the other apostles after they betook themselves to follow Christ, betook themselves to be fishermen too : for it is certain that the greater number of them were found together fishing by Jesus after his resurrection, as it is recorded in the 21st chapter of St. John's gospel, v. 3, 4. This was the employment of these happy fishermen, concerning which choice some have made these observations : first, that he never reproved these for their employment or calling as he did the scribes and the moneychangers ; and secondly, he found that the hearts of such men were fitted for contemplation and quietness, men of mild, and sweet, and peaceable spirits, as indeed most anglers are; these men our blessed Saviour, who is observed to love to plant grace in good natures, though indeed nothing be too hard for him, yet these men he chose to call from their irreprovable employment of fishing and gave them grace to be his disciples and to follow him and do wonders. I say four of twelve."

There I think we may safely rest the defence of our favorite sport, especially upon secondly; for it is all very well to say animals must be slain that we may live, and yet it does not give one a high idea of the fineness of the man who chooses the occupation of a butcher, and is happiest when he is killing something. Blood! Iago, blood! For my part, while recognizing the necessity that the sheep should bleat for the lamb slain that I may feast, I don't profess to see that the arrangement is anything to rave over as an illustration of the wisdom or the goodness of God. Let us eat, asking no questions, but trusting that some day we shall see clearly that all is well. Meanwhile I give up coursing, fox hunting, and pigeon shooting as unworthy sports, and never again will I kill a deer in sport. I once saw the mild, reproachful eyes of one turned upon me as it lay wounded, as much as to say: "I am so sorry it was *you* who did this." So was I, poor innocent thing. It is years since I saw that look, but it haunts me yet at intervals. It is one of the many things I have done for which I am ever sorry.

Too much fishing! It is no use to try to give you the good things of Izaak Walton, for it is with

him as with Shakespeare. Two volumes of his
"beauties" handed to gentle Elia. "This is all
very well, my friend, but where are the other five
volumes?" We must get out of Dovedale—that is
clear. *Allons done!*

Our stage to-day was to Chatsworth, twenty-four
miles, where our Fourth of July dinner was to be
celebrated. As we passed Ilam Hall we stopped,
sounded our horn, and gave three cheers for the
squire who had been so kind to his "American
cousins."

Our luncheon was beside the pretty brook at
Youlgreaves, on the estate of the Duke of Rutland,
and a beautiful trout-stream it is. We could see the
speckled beauties darting about, and were quite prepared to believe the wonderful stories told us of the
basketfuls taken there sometimes. There is something infectious in a running stream. It is the prettiest thing in nature. Nothing adds so much to our
midday enjoyment as one of these—

> "Making music o'er the enamelled stones,
> And giving a gentle kiss to every sedge
> It overtaketh in its pilgrimage."

Mother and Aggie were off to paidle in the burn
after luncheon, and as a fitting close they kilted their
petticoats and danced a highland reel on the greensward, in sight of the company, but at some distance
from us. They were just wee lassies again, and to
be a wee lassie at seventy-one is a triumph indeed;
but, as mother says, that is nothing. She intends to
be as daft for many years to come, for grandfather
was far older when he alarmed the auld wives of the

village on Halloween night, sticking his false face through the windows. "Oh!" said one, recovering from her fright, "it is just that daft callant, Andrew Carnegie!" I remember one day, in Dunfermline, an old man in the nineties—a picture of withered eld, a few straight, glistening white hairs on each side of his head, and his nose and chin threatening each other—tottered across the room to where I was sitting, and laying his long, skinny hand upon my head, murmured:

"An' ye're a gran'son o' Andrew Carnegie's! Aye, maan, I've seen the day when your grandfaether an' me could have hallooed ony reasonable maan oot o' his judgment."

I hope to be a daft callant at seventy-one—as daft as we all were that day. Indeed, we were all daft enough while coaching, but mother really ought to have been restrained a little. She went beyond all bounds.

Let me try to give an idea how this blessed England is crowded. Here is a signboard we stopped at to-day, to make sure we were taking the right way; for, even with the ordnance map upon one's knee, strict attention is required or you will be liable to take the wrong turn.

A voice from the general manager: "Perry, stop at the post and let us be sure."

"Right, sir."

The post points four ways, east, west, north, and south.

First arm reads as follows: Tissington, 3; Matlock Bath, 10; Chesterfield, 21.

Second arm: Ashbourne, 3; Derby, 16; Kissington, 19.

Third arm : Dovedale, Okedon, Ilam.

Fourth arm : New Haven, 6 ; Buxton, 17 ; Bakewell, 13 ; Chatsworth, 16.

All this the guide-post said at one turn, and fortunate it was that Chatsworth, our destination, happened to be upon the fourth arm, for had the worthy road-surveyors not deemed it necessary to extend their information beyond Bakewell, you see we might as well have consulted the Book of Days.

The entrance to Kissington estate was near the post, and we were very kindly permitted to drive through, which it was said would save several miles and give us a view of another English hall. We managed, however, to take a wrong turn somewhere, and added some eight miles to our journey ; so much the better—the longer the route the happier we were.

Every English hall seems to have some special features in which it surpasses all others. This is as it should be, for it permits every fortunate owner to love his own home for acknowledged merits of its own. If one has the nobler terrace, another boasts a finer lawn ; and if one has woods and a rookery, has not the other the winding Nith through its borders? One cannot have the best of everything, even upon an English estate ; neither can one life have the best possible of everything. Let us then be thankful for our special mercies, and let all our ducks be swans, as friend Edward says mine are.

Have you never had your friend praise his wife to you in moments of confidence, when you have been fishing for a week together? You wonder for a few moments, as you recall the Betsey or Susan he extols, for, if the truth is to be spoken, you have as it were shed tears for him when you thought of his yoke. Well, that is the true way : let him make her a swan, even if she is not very much of a duck.

We stopped at Rowsley for Miss French. She brought the London *Times*, which gave us the first news of the terrible catastrophe in Washington. We would not believe that the shot was to prove fatal. It did not seem possible that President Garfield's career was to end in such a way ; but, do what we could, the great fear would not down, and we reached Chatsworth much depressed. Our fourth of July was a sad one, and the intended celebration was given up. Fortunately, the news became more encouraging day after day, so much so that the coaching party ventured to telegraph its congratulations through Secretary Blaine, and it was not until we reached New York that we knew that a relapse had occurred. The cloud which came over us, therefore, had its silver lining in the promise of recovery and a return to greater usefulness than ever.

We stopped to visit Haddon Hall upon our way to Chatsworth, but here we came upon tourists' ground. Every one does the sights of the neighborhood, and readers are therefore respectfully referred to the guide-books. We had our first dusty ride to-day, for we are upon limestone roads, but the discomfort was only trifling ; the weather, however, was really warm, and our umbrellas were brought into use as sunshades.

Haddon Hall is a fine specimen of the old hall, and Chatsworth of the new, except that the latter partakes far too much of the show feature. It is no doubt amazing to the crowds of Manchester and Birmingham workers who flock here for a holiday and who have seen nothing finer, but to us who have in our travels seen the real gems of England, this Chatsworth is largely paste. I speak only of the interior, of course, for the house itself and its surroundings are grand.

EDENSOR, July 4.

Edensor is the model village which the Duke of Devonshire has built adjoining the park—a very appropriate and pretty name, for it is perhaps the finest made-to-order village in England. The day was so warm, and our next stage to Buxton being not very long (twenty-six miles), we decided to spend the day here and take an evening drive.

We met here, enjoying their honeymoon, a bride and groom who were well known to our Wolverhampton delegation, and how do you suppose they were travelling? Not in the ordinary mode, I assure you. I mention this incident that some of my charming young lady friends, who give me so much pleasure riding with me, may make a note of it. They were doing beautiful Derbyshire on horseback! It was delightful to see them start off in this way. I became interested in the bride, who must be no ordinary woman to think of this plan; she told me it was proving a wonderful success; and the happy young fellow intimated to me, in a kind of confidential way, that her novel idea was the finest one he had ever been a party to. I asked him if he could honestly recommend it, and he boldly said he could. We must think over this.

The evening ride was one of our pleasantest experiences. How entrancing England is after a warm day, when everything seems to rejoice in the hours of peace succeeding the sunshine which forces growth!

> "When the heart-sick earth
> Turns her broad back upon the gaudy sun,
> And stoops her weary forehead to the night
> To struggle with her sorrow all alone,
> The moon, that patient sufferer, pale with pain,
> Presses her cold lips on her sister's brow
> Till she is calm."

It is thus the earth appeared to me as we drove along; it was resting after its labors of the sunny day. The night was spent at Buxton, that famous spa. Many invalids are there drinking the waters; but I take it, as is usual with such places, the change of air and scene, of thought and effort, and, with most, change of diet and freedom from excess, count for ninety-nine points, and the waters, maybe, for one. But it is of no consequence what does it, so it is done, and Buxton continues to flourish. Our hotel was a magnificent "limited company" affair. The start next morning was a sight in the first real downpour in dead earnest we had experienced. The sky was dark—not one tiny ray of light to give us the slightest hope of change; the barometer low and still falling. Clearly we were in for it; nevertheless, at the appointed hour the Gay Charioteers, arrayed in their waterproofs, with the good hats and bonnets all inside the coach, passed through the crowds of guests who lined the hall, wondering at these mad Americans, and took their accustomed seats with an alacrity that showed they considered the weather "perfectly lovely."

There are two miles of steep ascent as we leave the town, and a few of us decided to walk, Misses Emma and Alice being of the number. Those who started upon the coach were all right; the pedestrians, however, found themselves far from dry when the top was reached—feet and knees were wet. By noon the rain had ceased, and we stopped at a little inn, where fires were made, our "reserve" clothing brought into use, and our wet clothes dried, and we were as happy as larks when we sat down to luncheon. Is not that a wise test which Thackeray puts in the mouth of one of his waiters : "Oh, I knew he was a gentleman, he was so easily pleased"? Well, our host and hostess at that little inn, who were taken so by surprise when a four-in-hand stopped at the door, said something like this about the American ladies and gentlemen as they left. Why not? Nothing comes amiss to the Gay Charioteers, and so on we go to Manchester, getting once more into the grim, smoky regions of manufacturing enterprise.

Manchester, July 6.

Mine host of The Queen's takes the prize for the one best "swell" dinner enjoyed by the party ; but then the rain and the moderate luncheon at the little inn, so different from the picnics on flowery banks, may have given it a relish. The Queen's was evidently determined that its American guests should leave with a favorable impression, and so they did.

There was time to visit the Town Hall and walk the principal streets, but all felt an invincible repugnance to large towns. It was not these we had come to see. Let us get away as soon as possible, and out once more to the green fields. The morning was cloudy, but the rain held off, and we left the hotel amid a great crowd. The police had at last to step in front of the coach and clear the way. The newspapers had announced our arrival and intended departure, and this brought the crowd upon us. Getting into and out of large cities is the most difficult part of our driving, for the ordnance map is useless there—frequent stoppages and inquiries must be made; but so far we have been fortunate, and our horn keeps opposing vehicles out of our way in narrow streets and in turning corners. We were bound for Anderton Hall, to spend the night with our friend Mr. Burroughs. Luncheon was taken in a queer, old-fashioned inn, where we ate from bare deal tables and drank home-brewed ale while we sang:

> "Let gentlemen fine sit down to their wine,
> But we will stick to our beer, we will,
> For we will stick to our beer."

The number and variety of temperance drinks advertised in England is incredible. Non-alcoholic beverages meet us in flaming advertisements at every step—from nervous tonics, phosphated, down to the most startling of all, which, according to the London *Echo* of June 2d, the Bishop of Exeter advertised when he opened a coffee-house, saying:

> "It looks like beer,
> It smells like beer,
> It tastes like beer,
> Yet it is not beer."

Better if it had been, your reverence, for your new beverage was probably a villainous compound, certain to work more injury than genuine beer. In this country we also try to cheat the devil. I mean our unco good people try it; but we call it "bitters," and the worse the whiskey the better the bitters.

CHORLEY, July 7.

As we approached Anderton Hall the English and American flags were seen floating from the archway, earnest of cordial welcome. We were quite at home immediately. Mr. and Mrs. Burroughs had their family and friends ready to greet us. The dining-hall was decorated with the flags of the old and the new lands, gracefully intertwined, symbolizing the close and warm friendship which exists between them—never, we hope, to be again disturbed. We had a long walk about the place and on the banks of the famous Rivington Reservoir, which supplies Manchester with water. In the evening, after dinner, came speeches. The evening passed delightfully. Next day we were sorely tempted. Mr. Middleton was to have the school-children at his house to be entertained, and an opportunity to see a novel celebration was afforded us. Our host and hostess were pressing in their invitation for us to stay, but one night of fourteen guests, two servants, and four horses, was surely enough; so we blew our horn, and, with three ringing cheers for Anderton Hall and

all within it, drove out of its hospitable gates. We
stopped and paid our respects to Mr. and Mrs. Middleton as we passed their place, and left them all
with very sincere regret. How pleasant it would
be to linger, but Inverness lies far in the north. We
are scarcely one-third of our way thither and the
time-table stares us in the face. We do not quite
"fold our tents like the Arabs and silently steal
away," but at the thrilling call of the horn we
mount, and with cheers and God-speeds take our departure for other scenes.

PRESTON, July 8.

Preston, sixteen miles away, is our destination,
permitting a late start to be made. Our route is still
through a manufacturing district, for Manchester
reaches her arms far out in every direction. We
pass every now and then a company of show-people
with their vans. Sometimes we find the caravan at
rest, the old, weary-looking horses nibbling the roadside grass, for the irregularity of the hedges in England gives fine little plots of grass along the hedgerows, and nice offsets, as it were, in the road, where
these strolling players, and gypsies, peddlers, and
itinerant venders of all sorts of queer things, can call
a halt and enjoy themselves. Every van appears to
be invested with an air of mystery, for was not our
Shakespeare,

"Th' applause, delight, the wonder of our stage,"

a strolling player, playing his part in barns and
outhouses to wondering rustics? There are such
possibilities in every van that I greet the sweet little

child as if she were a princess in disguise, and the dark-eyed, foreign-looking boy as if he might have within him the soul of Buddha. I do not believe that any other form of life has the attractions of this nomadic existence. To make it perfect one should put away enough in the funds as a reserve to be drawn upon when he could not make the pittance necessary to feed and clothe him and buy a few old copies of good books as he passed through a village. The rule might be, only when hungry shall this pocketbook be opened. I should have one other contingency in order to be perfectly happy—when I wanted to help a companion in distress. Elia was truly not very far from it. If I were not the independent gentleman I am, I would be a member of a strolling band such as we pass in this crowded land every now and then, and boast that Shakespeare was of our profession. What are the Charioteers after all in their happiest dream but aristocratic gypsies? That is the reason we are so enraptured with the life.

But in Preston there is no scope for idealism. It is a city where cotton is king. No town can be much less attractive; but, mark you, a few steps toward the river and you overlook one of the prettiest parks in the world. The Ribble runs at the foot of the sloping hill upon which the city stands, and its banks have been converted into the pleasure-ground I speak of, in which the toilers sport in thousands and gaze upon the sweet fields of living green beyond far into the country. It is not so bad when the entire district is not given over to manufactures, as in Birmingham and Manchester. There is the cloud, but there is the silver lining also.

At Preston many of us received letters from home. Harry's funny one from his little daughter Emma (a namesake of our Emma of the Charioteers) gave us a good laugh. I remember there was one announcement particularly noteworthy: "Ninety dollars gone to smash, papa. The pony's dead." There is your future special correspondent for you.

At eleven o'clock this evening the party received a notable addition—Andrew Martin, my old schoolfellow and "the Maester's son," arrived from Dunfermline. He was received at the station by a committee especially appointed for the purpose, and shortly thereafter duly initiated into all the rites and mysteries of the Gay Charioteers. He was required, late as it was, to sing two Scotch songs to determine his eligibility. There may be some man who can sing "Oh! why left I my hame?"— my favorite at present, and written by Gilfillan in Dunfermline, note that—or "When the kye come hame," better than our new member, but none of us has been so fortunate as to meet him, nor have I ever heard one who could sing them as well for me; but there may be a touch of Auld Lang Syne in his voice which strikes chords in my heart and sets them vibrating. There are subtle sympathies lurking in the core of man's nature, responsive to no law but their own, but I notice all press Andrew to sing, and keep very quiet when he does. We had the pleasure of seeing the new member get just as daft as the rest of us next day, gathering wild flowers along the hedgerows, the glittering, towering coach coming up to us. He had time to say: "Man, this canna be *vera* bad for us!" No, not very; only we did not know then how bad it would be for us when, after the dream-like existence had passed and we were back once more to our labors of this workaday world, thrown out as it were from a paradise and falling as Milton's Satan fell.

Fortunately we did not know then that for months after our fall there were to be only sad memories of days of happiness so unalloyed that they can never again be equalled. It is not at all desirable to be honestly persuaded that you never again can have seven weeks of such days as made us happy, innocent children; but we shall see. There are as good fish in the sea as were ever caught, and though it is true they do not seem to bite as they used to, maybe we can venture to try coaching again. The height of our musical season was during this part of the journey. Miss Reid, Miss Johns, and Mrs. King are all musical and blessed with the power of song. Messrs. Martin, McCargo, and King differ only as one star differs from another in glory; and there was another gentleman, who shall be nameless, who sang without being asked, and who, as usual, was not encored by his unappreciative audience.

Davie deserves notice. He sang a beautiful Scotch song to-day, "Cowden Knowes," and when he was done Andrew immediately asked: "Whaur did ye get that? Ye didna get that out of a book!"

Right, my boy. It was at his father's knee. Who ever learnt a Scotch song out of books? They are possessed of souls, these songs, to be caught only from living lips. The bodies alone are to be found within the bars.

Passing Bolton we saw the first bowling green,

sure proof that we are getting northward, where every village has its green and its bowling club, the ancient game of bowls still offering to rural England attractions paramount to more modern sports.

We lunched at Grisdalebrook, ten miles from Lancaster, which was to be our stopping-place. To-day's drive was made fragrant by the scent of new-mown hay, and we passed many bands of merry haymakers. When Dickens pronounced no smell the best smell, he must have momentarily forgotten that which so delighted us. I do give up most of the so-called fine smells, but there are a few better than Dickens's best, and surely that of to-day is of them. We went into a Catholic church in one of our strolls, for let it be remembered many a glorious tramp we had, and the coach was rarely honored with all the party when a chance to walk presented itself. The requests posted upon the door of this church seemed to carry one back a long way:

"Of your charity pray for the soul of Rebecca Robinson, who died June 7th, 1880, fortified with rites of Holy Church, on whose soul sweet Jesus have mercy. R. I. P."

There were several such requests. What a power that church has been and is only one who has travelled the world round can know. In England here it is but a sickly, foreign plant, so fearfully foreign. We can all repeat Buddha's words and apply them to it, but they should not stop here:

"And third came she who gives dark creeds their power,
Silabbat-paramâsa, sorceress,
Draped fair in many lands as lowly Faith,
But ever juggling souls with rites and prayers;

> The keeper of those keys which lock up Hells
> And open Heavens. 'Wilt thou dare?' she said,
> 'Put by our sacred books, dethrone our gods,
> Unpeople all the temples, shaking down
> That law which feeds the priests and props the realm?'
> But Buddha answered, 'What thou bidd'st me keep
> Is form which passes, but the free truth stands;
> Get thee unto thy darkness.'"

LANCASTER, July 9–10.

We had done our twenty-nine miles from Preston and reached Lancaster in good season. There we had a treat. The High Sheriff for the county had just been elected and made his entry into town according to immemorial custom. He represents royalty in the county during his term of office, which I believe is only two years. It costs the recipient of the honor a large sum to maintain the dignities of the office, for its emoluments are nil. The sheriff was staying at our hotel, a very fine one, The County. He is wakened every morning by two heralds richly dressed in the olden style and bearing halberds. They stand in front of the hotel and sound their bugles to call His Highness forth. It is the Lord Mayor's procession on a small scale. Nobody laughs outright at the curious mixture of feudal customs with this age's requirements, however much everybody may laugh in his sleeve; but England will have lost some picturesque features when all the shams are gone. If mankind were not greatly influenced by forms, I could wish that just enough of the "good old times"—which were very bad times indeed—could be preserved, if only to prove how far we had outgrown them; but every form and every sham, from royalty downward, carries its good or evil with it. That not only the substance should be right, but that the form should correspond truly to it, is to the last degree important; so I reconcile myself to the passing away of forms which no longer honestly represent what they imply.

Lancaster is a beautiful place and noted for its admirable charitable institutions. The lunatic asylum and an orphanage attracted our special attention. These and kindred institutions abound in England, and are ably conducted. Rich Englishmen do not leave their fortunes for uses of this kind as often as Americans do. The ambition to found a family, and the maintenance of an aristocratic class by means of primogeniture and entail, tend to divert fortunes from this nobler path into the meaner end of elevating a name in the social scale; but the general public in Britain is most generous, and immense sums in the aggregate are annually collected for charitable institutions. It is common for a class to support its own unfortunates. The commercial travellers, for instance, have an extensive home near London for children of their fellows and for members in their old age.

One cannot travel far in Britain without seeing that the British are a people most mindful of the unfortunate. These pretty homes of refuge and of rest we see scattered everywhere over the land, nor are they the least glorious of the many monuments of England's true worth.

A Mr. Ripley left his fortune for an orphanage, open to all orphan children born within fifteen miles of Lancaster. Three hundred are now provided for, but so rapidly has the fund grown that it has been found practicable to extend the boundaries of its beneficence, and children from distant Liverpool are now admitted. Bravo! Mr. Ripley. What is an earldom for your eldest son to this! His father's name will carry him farther with the best, and he should be prouder of it. Show me the earl who has done as much for his neighborhood.

Lancaster Castle is a noble one ; its gateway is not surpassed. Here John o' Gaunt hundreds of years ago put his finger upon the dire root of England's woes, as far as the land goes :

> "This dear, dead land,
> Dear for her reputation through the world,
> Is now *leased* out."

There you have it—this England is leased out. The soil is not worked by its owners, and never, till England changes its practice and can boast a peasant proprietary working its own acres in small farms, untrammelled by vicious laws, will she know what miracles can be wrought by those who call each little spot their own—their home. Englishmen are slow to change, but the day is not far distant when ownership of land will depend upon residence on it and its proper cultivation. Denmark's example will be followed. Cumulative taxes will be levied upon each number of acres beyond a minimum number, and large proprietors taxed out of existence as they have been in Denmark, to the country's good and nobody's injury. We tax a man who keeps racing-horses or who sports armorial bearings. It is the same principle : we can tax a man who keeps a larger amount of land than he can work to the State's advantage. The rights of property are all very well in their place, but the rights of man and the good of the commonwealth are far beyond them. I wish England would just let me arrange that little land matter for her. It would save her a generation of agitation.

Sunday was spent in Lancaster, and much enjoyed. The service in church was fine and the afternoon's excursion to the country delightful. Here Miss Amelia Bantock and Mr. Dickinson left us after receiving the blessing of the party. Miss Graham and Miss Dickinson, who were to join us here, failed us, but we fortunately found them waiting at Kendall. We started for that town, twenty-two miles distant, on Monday morning. It is the entrance to the celebrated Lake District. Messrs. Thorn and Middleton, whom we had met at Anderton Hall, passed us before we reached Lancaster on Saturday, on bicycles. They were out for a run of a hundred and five miles that day, to visit friends beyond that city. We meet such travellers often. Their club now numbers seven thousand members. For an annual payment of half a crown (62 cents), a member has lists of routes and hotels sent him for any desired district, with the advantage of reduced charges. It is nothing to do a hundred miles per day; many have done London to Bath, two hundred miles, within the twenty-four hours.

The country swarms with these fellows. I saw fifteen hundred in Bushy Park one day at a meet. I think seventy-five clubs were there, each in a different uniform. Bicycles are also growing in use for practical purposes, and many post-routes in the country are served by men who use these machines. But it takes roads like the English, and a level country, to do much with them.

Our evening was spent in visiting the ruined castle and admiring a pretty Japanese kind of garden, so much in so little space, which attracted our attention as we passed. The owner, Mr. Thompson, a solicitor, kindly invited us in, and afterward showed us his house. We are always receiving kindnesses from all sorts and conditions of men.

Next day, July 12th, our objective point was Grassmere, eighteen miles away. Such a lovely morning! but, indeed, we are favored beyond measure with superb weather all the time. This stage in our progress introduced us to the scenery of the lakes, and we all felt that it deserved its Wordsworth; but were we ever to let loose and enter the descriptive, where would it lead? This is the rock upon which many a fair venture in story-telling has suffered shipwreck. Great mountains always carry one upward, but these are not great, nor is there anything great in the region. All is very sweet and pleasing and has its own peculiar charm, like the school of Lake Poets.

At Bowness, about midway of the lake, we left the coach for the first time for any other kind of conveyance. After enjoying a rare treat in a sail up and down the lake in the pretty steamer, we rejoined the coach at Ambleside, where we had ordered it to await us.

Passing Storr's Hall, the mind wandered back to the meeting there of Wordsworth, Southey, Coleridge, Christopher North, and greater than all, our Walter Scott; and surely not in all the earth could a fitter spot than this have been found for their gathering. How much the world of to-day owes to the few names who spent days together here! Not often can you say of one little house, "Here had we our country's honor roofed," to so great an extent as it would be quite allowable to say in this instance. But see the vanity of human aspirations! If there was one wish dearer than another to the greatest of these men, it was that Abbotsford should remain from generation to generation the home of his race. This very hour, while sailing on the lake, a newspaper was handed to me, and my eye caught the advertisement, "Abbotsford to let," followed by the stereotyped description, so many reception-rooms, nursery, outbuildings, and offices, suitable for a gentleman's establishment. Shade of the mighty Wizard of the North, has it come to this! Oh, the pity of it! the pity of it! Well for your fame that you built for mankind other than this stately home of your pride. It will crumble and pass utterly away long before the humble cot of Jeannie Deans shall fade from the memory of man. The time will come when the greatest will be as much forgot

> "As the canoe that crossed a lonely lake
> A thousand years ago."

But even the New Zealander who stands on the ruins of London Bridge will know something of Walter Scott if he knows much worth knowing. "Abbotsford to let!" This to come to me just as we were passing one of the haunts of Scott, than whom no greater Scot ever lived save one. Fortunately no such blow is possible for the memory of Burns.

> "After life's fitful fever, he sleeps well;
> Treason has done his worst: nor steel, nor poison,
> Malice domestic, ... nothing,
> Can touch him further!"

For this let us be thankful. We visited Wordsworth's grave reverently in the twilight. Fresh, very fresh flowers lay upon it. God bless the hand that strewed them there this day! I think the following the one very great thing he gave the world: It contains "the golden guess which ever is the morning star to the full round of truth." The thought of the age—whether right or wrong we need not discuss—is hitherward:

> "For I have learned
> To look on Nature, not as in the hour
> Of thoughtless youth; but hearing oftentimes
> The still, sad music of humanity,
> Not harsh nor grating, though of ample power
> To chasten and subdue. And I have felt
> A presence that disturbs me with the joy
> Of elevated thoughts: a sense sublime
> Of something far more deeply interfused,
> Whose dwelling is the light of setting suns,
> And the round ocean, and the living air,
> And the blue sky, and in the mind of man
> A motion and a spirit that impels
> All thinking things, all objects of all thought,
> And rolls through all things."

There's a platform upon which this sceptical age may eventually stand. It is not materialistic and it is not dogmatic; perhaps it is the golden mean between extremes. I commend its teachings to both sides of the cocksure disputants, one of whom knows it is all just so, and the other as presumptuously knows there is nothing to know. Let them shake hands and await patiently the coming of clearer light, and get together in solid work here. Surely there is enough to keep them busy. We still " see through a glass darkly."

We spent our night at Grassmere, and had a fine row upon the lake.

GRASSMERE, July 13.

"Right, Perry!" Off for Keswick, only twelve miles distant; but who wants to hurry away from scenes like these? It rained heavily through the night, but is grand for us this morning. The mist was on the mountains though, and the clouds passed slowly over them, wrapping the tops in their mantle. The numerous rills dashing down the bare mountains were the themes of much praise. They reminded me of two fine verses from the " Light of Asia" upon " Being's ceaseless tide " :

> " Which, ever-changing, runs, linked like a river
>   By ripples following ripples, fast or slow—
> The same, yet not the same—from far-off fountains
>   To where its waters flow
> Into the seas. These, steaming to the sun,
>   Give the lost wavelets back in c'oudy fleece
> To trickle down the hills, and glide again ;
>   Knowing no pause or peace."

We seem to be miraculously protected from rain. Many times it has poured during the night, and yet the days have been perfect. " Carnegie weather" begins to be talked about, and we are all disposed to accept the inference that the fair goddess Fortune has fallen deep in love with us, since Prosperity seems to be our page during this journey.

The influence of America and of American ideas upon England is seen in various ways. We meet frequently one who has visited the Republic, whose advanced ideas, in consequence of the knowledge derived from actual contact with American affairs, are very decidedly proclaimed. The coaches in the Lake District have now the English and the American flags upon their sides, and we often see the Stars and Stripes displayed at hotels. Our present hostelry has a flaming advertisement ending with: "Patrons — Royalty and American Presidents." There must be slender grounds for both claims, I fancy. General Grant, however, may have been there. As the elected of the largest division of the English-speaking race, he no doubt outranked all other patrons.

At luncheon to-day it was found that our drinkables had better be cooled in the brook—an unusual performance this for England; but how vividly this little incident brings to mind the happy scene—the row of bottles in the stream, sticking up their tiny heads as if resentful at the extraordinary bath. Do not imagine that our party were worse to water than to corn; sixteen hungry people need a good many bottles of various kinds, for we had many tastes to gratify. We were all temperance people, however— a few of us even total abstinence, who required special attention.

At Keswick I wandered round the principal square and laughed at the curious names of the inns there. In this region inns abound. Almost every house in that square offered entertainment for man and beast. Here is a true copy of names of inns noted in a few squares in the village : Fighting Cocks, Packhorse, Red Lion, Dog and Duck, Black Lion, Deerhound, White Hart, Green Lion, Pig and Whistle, White Lion, Black Bull, Elephant and Castle, Lamb and Lark, The Fish. If the whole village were scanned there would be beasts enough commemorated in its inns to make a respectable menagerie. Indeed, for that one Green Lion, Barnum might safely pay more than for Jumbo.

The names of English inns we have seen elsewhere are equally odd; let me note a few : Hen and Chickens, Dog and Doublet, King and Crown, Hole in the Wall, Struggling Man, Jonah and the Ark, Angel and Woolsack, Adam and Eve, Rose and Crown, Crown and Cushion. We laughed at one with an old-fashioned swinging sign, upon which a groom was scrubbing away at a naked black man (you could almost hear his pruss, pruss, pruss). The name of the house was " Labor in Vain Inn"—a perfect illustration, no doubt, in one sense ; in the higher sense, not so. Under the purifying influences of equality, found only in republican institutions, America has taught the world she can soon make white men out of black. Her effort to change the slave into a freeman has been anything but labor in vain ; what is under the skin can be made white enough always, if we go at it with the right brush. None genuine unless stamped with the well-known brand " Republic." " All men are born free and *equal*" warranted to cure the most desperate cases when all other panaceas fail, from a mild monarchy up to a German despotism. To be well shaken, however, before taken, and applied internally, externally, and eternally, like Colonel Sellers' eye-wash.

Harry and I were absent part of this day, having run down to Workington to see our friend Mr. Gardiner, at the Steel Rail Mills. Pardon us!— this was our only taste of business during the trip; never had the affairs of this world, or of any other for that matter, been so completely banished from our thoughts. To get back to blast-furnaces and rolling-mills was distressing; but we could not well pass our friend's door, so to speak. We have nothing to say about manufacturing, for it is just with that as with their political institutions: England keeps about a generation behind, and yet deludes herself with the idea that she is a leader among nations. The truth is she is not even a good follower where others lead, but exceptions must be noted here: a few of her ablest men are not behind America in manufacturing, for there are one, or perhaps two, establishments in England which lead America. A great race is the British when they do go to work and get rid of their antiquated prejudices. Visitors to America like Messrs. Howard, Lothian Bell, Windsor Richards, Martin, and others, have no prejudices which stick. Let Uncle Sam look out. If he thinks John Bull will remain behind in the industrial or the political race either, I do not; and I believe when he sets to work in earnest he cannot be beaten. The Republic of England, when it comes, will excel all other republics as much as the English monarchy has excelled all other monarchies, or as much as Windsor Richards' steel practice and plant excel any we can boast of here at present. It is our turn now to take a step forward, unless we are content to be beaten. This is all right. Long may the two branches of the family stimulate each other to further triumphs, the elder encouraging us to hold fast that which is good, the younger pointing the way upward and onward—a race in which neither can lose, but in which both must win! Clear the course! Fair play and victory to both!

The annual public debate of University College, London, attracted our notice to-day before leaving Kendal. The subject debated was: "That the advance of Democracy in England will tend to strengthen the Foundations of Society."

Lord Rosebery presided, and it is his speech at the close which possesses political significance as coming from one who wears his rank

"For the sake of liberal uses
And of great things to be done,"

and of whom almost any destiny may be predicted if he hold the true course. He said:

"As regards government, there seemed to be great advantage in democracy. With an oligarchy the responsibility was too great and the penalty for failure too high. He did not share the asperity manifested by one of the speakers against American institutions, and, having visited the country on several occasions, he felt the greatest warmth for America and the American people. Persons who elected by free choice a moderate intellect to represent them were better off than those who had a leviathan intellect placed over them against their will, and this free choice the people of the United States possessed.

It had been said by the opponents of democracy that the best men in America devoted themselves to money-getting; but this was a strong argument in its favor, as showing that democracy was not correctly represented as a kind of grabbing at the property of others."

Never were truer words spoken than these, my lord. What a pity you were not allowed the privilege of starting "at scratch" in life's race, like Gladstone or Disraeli. From any success achieved there must be made the just deduction for so many yards allowed *Lord* Rosebery. Receive the sincere condolences of him who welcomed you to honorary membership of the Burns Club of New York—not because of these unfortunate, unfair disadvantages, for he would not have welcomed a prince for his rank, but for your merits as a man.

We reached Penrith July 14th, after a delightful day's drive. Never were the Gay Charioteers happier, for the hilly ground gave us many opportunities for grand walks. When these come it is a red-letter day. The pleasure of walking should rank as one of the seven distinct pleasures of existence, and yet I have some friends who know nothing of them; they are not coaching through England, however.

I have omitted to chronicle the change that came over the Queen Dowager shortly after we started from Wolverhampton; till then she had kept the seat of honor next to Perry, inviting one after another as a special honor to sit in front with her. She soon discovered that a good deal of the fun going on was missed; besides, she had not all of us under her eye. Her seat was exchanged for the middle of the back form, where she was supported by one on each side, while four others had their faces turned to hers, giving an audience of no less than six for her stories and old ballads. Her tongue went from morning till night, if I do say it, and her end of the coach was always in for its share of any frolic stirring. She was "in a gale" all day to-day, and kept us all roaring.

PENRITH, July 14.

Our next stage would take us to Carlisle, the border-town behind which lay the sacred soil. Mr. Burroughs and his son joined us here and went on with us the last day upon English soil, waving adieu, as it were, as we plunged into Scotland. Mr. and Mrs. King left us for Paisley to see the children, and what a loss I here record no one but the members can possibly understand. Aaleck and Aggie gone! If anything could long dampen the joyous spirits of the party, this separation surely would have done it; but we were to meet again in Edinburgh, where the reconstruction of the Charioteers was to take place. At Carlisle, too, the Parisians were to be welcomed back again -plenty to look forward to, you see. We started for Carlisle July 15th, the day superb as usual.

We had left the Lake District, with its hills and flowing streams, to pass through a tamer land; but our luncheon to-day, in a field near " Hesketh in the Forest," was not unromantic. The members from Anderton Hall caught the fever, as was usual with neophytes, and regretted that their return was imperatively required. One day gave them a taste of the true gypsy life.

CARLISLE, July 15.

Here is reconstruction for you with a vengeance! First, let us mourn the unhappy departures: Mr. and Mrs. King went yesterday, and Miss Reid, Miss Graham, the Misses Bantock, Miss Dickinson, and Mr. Burroughs and son go to-day. Cousin Maggie, who had become absorbed in this kind of life, so dazed with happiness, her turn has come too, even she must go; Andrew Martin, with his fine Scotch aroma and his songs, must report to his superior officer at the encampment, for is he not a gallant volunteer and an officer under Her Majesty, "sworn never to desert his home except in case of invasion"! Well, we cannot help these miserable changes in this world, nor the "sawt, sawt tears" of the young ladies as they kiss each other, swearing eternal friendship, and sob good-byes.

But if farewell ever sighs, welcome comes in smiling. Look! Cousin Eliza in my arms and a warm kiss taken! That is the very best of consolation. Clever, artistic Miss Roxburgh, too, from Edinburgh; and then are we not to have our four originals back again, after two long weeks' absence! It was a fortunate thing that our sad farewells were so promptly followed by smiling welcomes.

Do any people love their country as passionately as the Scotch? I mean the earth of it, the very atoms of which its hills and glens are composed. I doubt it. Now here is Maggie, a douce, quick, sensible girl. I tried to say something cheery to her to-day as we were approaching Carlisle, where we were to part, reminding her jokingly that she had received five weeks' coaching while her poor sister

Eliza would have only two. "Ah! but she has Scotland, Naig!" "Do you really mean to tell me that you would rather have two weeks in your own country than five weeks seeing a new land, and that land England, with London and Brighton, and the lakes and all?" I just wish you could have seen and heard how the "Of course" came in reply. The Scotch always have Scotland first in their hearts, and some of them, I really believe, will get into trouble criticising Paradise if it be found to differ materially from Scotland.

To-morrow we are to enter that land of lands. Fair England, farewell! How graciously kind has been the reception accorded by you to the wanderers! How beautiful you are! how tenderly dear you have become to all of us! Not one of us but can close our eyes and revel in such quiet beauty as never before was ours.

> "Not a grand nature . . .
> On English ground
> You understand the letter . . . ere the fall
> How Adam lived in a garden. All the fields
> Are tied up fast with hedges, nosegay like ;
> The hills are crumpled plains—the plains pastures,
> And if you seek for any wilderness
> You find at best a park. A nature
> Tamed and grown domestic . . .
> A sweet familiar nature, stealing in
> As a dog might, or child, to touch your hand,
> Or pluck your gown, and humbly mind you so
> Of presence and affection."

"There is no farewell to scenes like thine." From the depths of every heart in our company comes the trembling "God bless you, England!"

SCOTLAND.

> "Away, ye gay landscapes, ye gardens of roses!
>   In you let the minions of luxury rove;
> Restore me the rocks where the snowflake reposes,
>   Though still they are sacred to freedom and love:
> Yet, Caledonia, beloved are thy mountains,
>   Round their white summits though elements war;
> Though cataracts foam 'stead of smooth flowing fountains,
>   I sigh for the valley of dark Loch na Garr."

It was on Saturday, July 16th, that we went over the border, Mr. Wilson, the coach-owner, going with us, on his way to his native town.

The bridge across the boundary-line was soon reached. When midway over a halt was called, and vent given to our enthusiasm. With three cheers for the land of the heather, shouts of "Scotland forever," and the waving of hats and handkerchiefs, we dashed across the border. And, oh Scotland, my own, my native land, your exiled son returns with love for you as ardent as ever warmed the heart of man for his country. It's a God's mercy I was born a Scotchman, for I do not see how I could ever have been contented to be anything else. The little plucky dour deevil, set in her own ways and getting them too, level-headed and shrewd, with an eye to the main chance always and yet so lovingly weak, so fond, so led away by song or story, so easily touched to fine issues, so leal, so true! Ah! you suit me, Scotia, and proud am I that I am your son.

We stopped at Gretna Green, of course, and walked to the site of the famous blacksmith-shop, where so many romantic pairs have been duly joined in the holy bonds of wedlock. A wee laddie acted as guide, and from him we had our first real broad Scotch. His dialect was perfect. He brought wee Davie to mind at once. I offered him a shilling if he could "screed me aff effectual calling." He knew his catechism, but he could not understand it. Never mind that, Davie, that is another matter. Older heads than yours have bothered over that doctrine and never got to the bottom of it. Besides there will be a "revised edition" of that before you are a man. Just you let it alone; it is the understanding of that and some other dogmas of poor ignorant man's invention that thin the churches of men who think and "make of sweet religion a rhapsody of words." "But do you ken Burns?" "Aye," said Davie, "I ken 'A man's a man for a' that,' and 'Auld Lang Syne.'" "Good for you, Davie, there's another shilling. Good-bye! But I say, Davie, if you can't possibly remember all three of these pieces, don't let it be 'A man's a man for a' that' that you forget, for Scotchmen will need to remember that one of these days when we begin to set things to rights in earnest and demand the same right for prince, peer, and peasant. Don't let it be 'Auld Lang Syne' either, for there is more of 'Peace and Good-will upon Earth,' the essence of true religion, in that grand song, than in your effectual calling, Davie, my wee mannie. At least there is one who thinks so." Davie got my address, and said maybe he would come to America when he grew to be a man. I promised to give him a chance if he had not forgotten Burns, which is all we can do in the republic, where merit is the only road to success. We may make a Republican out of him yet, and have him return to his fellows to preach the equality of man, the sermon Scotland needs.

We lunched at Annan. It was at first decided that we had better be satisfied with hotel accommodations, as the day though fine was cool, with that little nip in the air which gives it the bracing quality ; but after we had entered the hotel the sun burst forth, and the longing for the green fields could not be overcome. We walked through the village across the river, and found a pretty spot in a grove upon high ground commanding extensive views up and down the stream, and there we gave our new members their first· luncheon. It would have been a great pity had we missed this picnic, for it was in every respect up to the standard. I laugh as I recall the difficulties encountered in selecting the fine site. The committee had fixed upon a tolerably good location in a field near the river, but this knoll was in sight, and we were tempted to go to it. We had gone so far from the hotel where the coach was, that Perry and Joe had to get a truck to bring the hampers. I remember seeing them pushing it across the bridge and up against the wall over which most of us had clambered. When mother's turn came the wall was found to be rather too much for her, but our managers were versatile. The truck was brought into requisition, and mother having mounted upon it was safely drawn from its platform over the wall. I stood back and could do nothing for laughter, but mother, who was not to be daunted, went over amid the cheers of the party. It was resolved, however, to be a little more circumspect in future ; wall-climbing at seventy-one has its limits.

Here is the bridge built by that worthy man and excellent representative of what is best in Scottish character in lowly life, James Carlyle—an honest brig destined to stand and never shame the builder. I remember how proudly Carlyle speaks of his father's work. No sham about either the man or his work, as little as there was in his more famous son.

Many have expressed surprise at Carlyle's Reminiscences, at the gnarled, twisted oak they show, prejudiced here, ill-tempered there. What did such people expect, I wonder. A poor, reserved, proud Scotch lad, who had to fight his way against the grim devils of poverty and neglect, of course he is twisted and "thrawn"; but a grand, tough oak for all that, as sound, stanch timber as ever grew, and Scotch to the core. Did any one take you, Thomas Carlyle, for a fine, symmetrical sycamore, or a graceful clinging vine? I think the Reminiscences, upon the whole, a valuable contribution to literature. Nor has Carlyle suffered in my estimation from knowing so much of what one might have expected. But will these critics of a grand individuality be kind enough to tell us when we shall look upon his like again, or where is another Jenny Carlyle to come from? She is splendid! The little tot who "blooded a laddie's nose" with her closed fist and conquered "the lubbley jock." This was in her early childhood's days, and look at her woman's work for Carlyle if you want a pattern for wives, my young lady friends, at least as a bachelor pictures wifehood at its best. The story told of Mr. Black's meeting with Carlyle should be true, if it be not. "Oh, Mr. Black," exclaimed Carlyle, "I'm glad to see ye, man. I've read some of yer books; they're vera amusin'; ye ken Scotch scenery well; but when are ye goin' to do some *wark*, man?" Great work did the old man do in his day, no doubt; but they also work who plant the roses, Thomas, else were we little better than the beasts of the field. Carlyle did not see this.

DUMFRIES, July 16-17.

We were at Dumfries for Sunday. We had just got housed at the hotel and sat down to dinner when we heard a vehicle stop, and running to the window saw our anxiously expected Parisians at the door. Hurrah! welcome! welcome! Once more united, never to part again till New York was reached! It was a happy meeting and there was much to tell upon both sides, but the coachers evidently had the better of it. The extreme heat encountered in France had proved very trying. Jeannie and Ben were tired out, Mr. and Mrs. McCargo looked somewhat better, for they had been a few days among Davie's "forbears" in the South of Scotland and had recuperated. Jeannie vividly expressed her feelings thus, when asked how she had enjoyed life since she left the Ark: "*Left* the Ark! I felt as if I had been poked out of it like the dove to find out about the weather, and had found it rough. When I lose sight of the coach again just let me know it!" We, on our part, were very glad to get our pretty little dove back, and promised that she should never be sent forth from among us again. One becomes confused at Dumfries, there is so much to learn. We are upon historic ground in the fullest sense, and so crowded too with notable men and events. Bruce slew the Red Comyn here in the church of the Minorite Friars; Admirable Crichton, Paul Jones, Allan Cunningham, Carlyle, Neilson of the Hot Blast, Patterson, founder of the Bank of England, and Miller of the steamship, are all of the district; and still another, a Scotch minister, was the founder of savings banks. While not forgetting to urge his flock to lay up treasures in another world, he did not fail to impress upon them a like necessity of putting by a competence for this one, sensible man! How many ministers leave behind them as powerful an agency for the improvement of the masses as this Dumfries man, the Rev. Mr. Duncan, has in savings banks? All the speculative opinions about the other world which man can indulge in are as nothing to the acquisition of those good, sober, steady habits which render possible upon the part of the wage-receiving class a good deposit in that minister's savings bank. The Rev. Mr. Duncan is my kind of minister, one who works much and preaches little. There is room for more of his kind.

It is to Dumfries we are also indebted for the steamship, as far as Britain's share in that crowning triumph is concerned, for upon Dalwinston Lake Miller used the first paddles turned by steam. The great magician also has waved his wand over this district. Ellangowan Castle, Dirk Hatteraick's Cave, and even Old Mortality himself are all of Dumfries; and as for Burns there is more of his best work there than anywhere else, and there he lies at rest with the thistle waving over him, fit mourner for Scotland's greatest son, and of all others the one he would have chosen. How he loved it! Think of his lines about the emblem dear, written while still a boy.

I wanted to stay a week in Dumfries, and I deemed myself fortunate to be able to spend Sunday there. Two Dunfermline gentlemen now resident there, Messrs. Reid and Alston, were kind enough to call upon us and offer their services. This was thoughtful and pleased me much. Accordingly on Sunday morning we started with Mr. Reid and did the town, Maxwelton Braes, Burns's house, and last his grave. None of us had ever been there before, and we were glad to make the pilgrimage. Horace Greeley (how he did worship Burns!) has truly said that of the thousands who yearly visit Shakespeare's birthplace, most are content to engrave their names with a diamond upon the glass, but few indeed leave the resting-place of the ploughman without dropping a tear upon the grave; for of all men be it was who nestled closest to the bosom of humanity. It is true that of all the children of men Burns is the best beloved. Carlyle knew him well, for he said Burns was the Æolian harp of nature against which the rude winds of adversity blew, only to be transmitted in their passage into heavenly music.

I think these are the two finest things that have been said about our idol, or about any idol, and I believe them to be deserved. So did Carlyle and Greeley, for they were not flatterers. Of what other human being could these two things be truly said? I know of none.

Our friends, Mr. and Mrs. Nelson, are the fortunate owners of Friars Carse estate. They called upon us Sunday noon, and invited us to dine with them that evening. A delegation from the party accepted, and were much pleased with their visit. Friars Carse is a lovely spot. The winding Nith is seen at its best from the lawn. As we drove past on Monday, morning we stopped and enjoyed a morning visit to our friends, who were exceedingly kind. Mr. Nelson has earned the grateful remembrance of every true lover of Burns by restoring the heritage and guarding with jealous care every vestige of one of the half dozen geniuses which the world will reverence more and more as the years roll by. He has wisely taken out the window upon the panes of which Burns wrote with a diamond, "Thou whom chance may hitherto lead," one of my favorites. This is now preserved, to be handed down as an heirloom in the family, finally to find its place in some public collection. While we were in the mansion a grand-daughter of Annie Laurie actually came in. I know of no young lady whose grandmother is so widely and favorably known. We were all startled to be brought so near to the ideal Annie Laurie of our dreams. It only shows that the course of true love never runs smooth when we hear that she did not marry the poetic lover. Well, maybe she was happier with a dull country squire. Poets are not proverbially model husbands ; the better poet, the worse husband, and the writer of Annie Laurie had the temperament pretty well developed.

Right, Perry ! We are off for Sanquhar, twenty-eight miles away ; the day superb, with a freshness unknown in the more genial south we are rapidly leaving behind. What a pretty sight it was to see Miss Nelson bounding along upon her horse in the distance, an avant courier leading us to a warm welcome at her beautiful home! Would I had been with her on Habeebah! We spent an hour or two there, and then with three enthusiastic cheers for "Friars Carse and a' within it," the Charioteers drove off; but long must fond recollections of that estate and of the faces seen there linger in our memories as among the most pleasing of our ever-memorable journey. A home upon the Nith near Dumfries has many attractions indeed. Our drive to-day lay along the Nith and through the Duke of Buccleugh's grounds to his noble seat Drumlanrig Castle. Here we have a real castle at last, none of your imported English affairs, as tame as caged tigers. How poor and insignificant they all seem to such as this! You want the moors, the hills and glens, and all the flavor of feudal institutions to give a castle its dignity and impress you with the thoughts of bygone days. Modern castles in England built to order are only playthings, toys; but in Scotland they are real and stir the chords. You cannot have in England a glen worthy of the name, with its dark amber-brown, foaming, rushing torrent dashing through it. We begin to feel the exhilarating influences of the north as we drive on, and to understand its charm. Byron says truly:

> "England! thy beauties are tame and domestic
> To one who has roamed on the mountains afar.
> Oh, for the crags that are wild and majestic!
> The steep frowning glories of dark Loch na Garr."

This was the feeling upon the coach to-day. My

eyes watered now and then and my heart beat faster as the grandeur of the scenery and the influences around came into play. This was my land, England only a far-off connection, not one of the family. "And what do you think of Scotland noo?" was often repeated. "The grandest day yet!" was said more than once as we drove through the glen ; but this has been said so often during this wonderful expedition, and has so often been succeeded by a day which appeared to excel its famous predecessor, that we are careful now to emphasize the yet ; for indeed we feel that there is no predicting what glories Scotland has in store for us beyond.

Our luncheon to-day was taken upon the banks of the Nith, an exquisitely beautiful spot. There was no repressing our jubilant spirits that day, and sitting there on Nith's banks the party burst into song, and one Scotch song followed another. There was a strange stirring of the blood, an exaltation of soul unknown before. The pretty had been left behind, the sublime was upon us. There was a nip in the air unfelt in the more genial climate of the south. The land over which brooded peace and quiet content had been left behind, that of the " mountain and the flood " was here, whispering of its power, swaying us to and fro and bending us to its mysterious will. In the sough of the wind comes the call of the genii to mount to higher heights, that we may exult in the mysteries of the mountain and the glen,

"The steep frowning glories of dark Loch na Garr."

Even our songs had the wail of the minor key suggesting the shadows of human life, eras of storm and strife, of heroic endurance and of noble sacrifice; the struggle of an overmatched people contending for generations against fearful odds and maintaining through all vicissitudes a distinctively national life. That is what makes a Scotchman proud of this peculiar little piece of earth, and stirs his blood and fills his eyes as he returns to her bosom. I wish poor Ireland could only fight now as Scotland did then. There would soon be an end of the Irish question, for then England would as soon attempt to impose English ideas upon that oppressed land as she would try to force them upon Scotland, and she would "as lief face the devil himself" as Scotland upon such an issue. Na, she must be "strokit canny wi' the hair," or there will be trouble, mark you!

We rested over Monday night, July 18th, at Sanquhar, a long one-main-street village, whose little inn could not accommodate us all, but the people were kind, and the gentlemen of the party had no cause to complain of their quarters. It was here that the minister absolved the Cameronians from allegiance to "the ungodly king"—a great step. Those sturdy Cameronians probably knew little of Shakespeare, but I fancy the speech of that rebel minister could not have been better ended, or begun either, than with the outburst of Laertes to another wicked king:

"I'll not be juggled with :
To hell, allegiance!"

Bravo! They would not be juggled with King Charles, neither will their descendants be, if any king hereafter is ever rash enough to try his "imperial" notions upon them. That day is past, thanks to that good minister and his Cameronians. I gazed upon the monument erected to these worthies, and gratefully remembered what the world owes to them.

We stepped into a stationer's shop there and met a character. One side of the shop was filled with the publications of the Bible Society, the other with drugs. "A strange combination this," I remarked.

"Weel, man, no sae bad. Pheseek for the body an' pheseek for the soul. Castor oil and Bibles no sae bad."

Harry and I laughed.

"Have you the revised edition here yet?" I inquired.

"Na, na, the auld thing here. Nane of yer new-fangled editions of the Scripture for us. But I hear they've shortened the Lord's Prayer. Noo, that's no a bad thing for them as hae to get up early in the mornins."

He was an original, and we left his shop smiling at his way of putting things. Scotland is the land of odd characters.

SANQUHAR, July 8.

We are off for Old Cumnock, the entire village seemingly out to see the start. Sanquhar on the moors does not seem to have many attractions, but last evening we had one of our finest walks. There is a fine deep glen hid away between the hills, with a torrent rushing through it, over which bridges have been thrown. We were tempted to go far up the glen. The long gloaming faded away into darkness and we had a weird stroll home. It was after ten o'clock when we reached the hotel. This may be taken as a specimen of our evenings; there is always the long walk in the gloaming after dinner, which may be noted as one of the rare pleasures of the day.

Our luncheon to-day could not be excelled, and in some features it was unique. The banks of Douglas Water was the site chosen. The stream divides, and a green island seemed so enchanting that the committee set about planning means to cross to it. The steps of the coach formed a temporary bridge over which the ladies were safely conducted, but not without some danger of a spill. As many as thirty school children, then enjoying their summer vacation, followed, and after a while ventured to fraternize with us. Such a group of rosy, happy little ones it would be difficult to meet with out of Scotland. Children seem to flourish without care in this climate. The difference between the children of America and Britain is infinitely greater than that between the adults of the two countries. Scotch children learn to pronounce as the English do in the schools, but in their play the ancient Doric comes out in full force. It is all broad Scotch yet in conversation. This will no doubt change in time, but it seemed to us that so far they have lost very few of the Scotch words and none of the accent. We asked the group to appoint one of their number to receive some money to buy "sweeties" for the party. Jeannie Morrison was the lassie proposed and unanimously chosen. Jeannie was in the sixth standard. In answer to an inquiry, it was at first said that no one else of the party was so far advanced, but a moment's consultation resulted in a prompt correction, and then came: "Aye, Aggie McDonald is too." But not one of the laddies was beyond the fifth. Well, the women of Scotland always were superior to the men. If a workingman in Scotland does not get a clever managing wife (they are helpmeets there), he never amounts to anything, and many a stupid man pulls up well through the efforts of his wife. It is much the same as in France.

The shyness of these children surprised our Americans much. They could scarcely be induced to partake of cakes and jelly, which must be rare delicacies with them. I created a laugh by insisting that even after I had been in America several years I was as shy as any of these children. My friends were apparently indisposed to accept such an assertion entirely, but an appeal to Davie satisfied them of my modesty in early youth. "*Ah, then!*" said Miss Maud. But this was cruel. I can safely appeal to Robert Pitcairn, even if he is a great railway magnate now, whether he has not a grudge yet for a dinner I made him lose when he was ravenous (as indeed I was myself), because I could not be induced to eat in a strange house. Mrs. Franciscus knows too, and often speaks of it, that I was the shyest boy she ever had to coax into feeling at home.

We left some rare morsels for these children when they had done cheering us at our departure. I warrant they "were nae blate." The dear little innocent, happy things! I wish I could get among them again. What would not one give to get a fresh start, to be put back a child again, that he might make such a record as seems possible when looking backward. How many things he would do that he did not do, how many he would not do that he did do! I sympathize with Faust, the offer was too tempting to be successfully withstood. It always seems to me that parents and others having charge of children might do more than is done to teach them the only means of making life worth living, and to point out to them the rocks and eddies from which they themselves have suffered damage in life's passage.

With the cheers of the children ringing in our ears we started on our way. While stopping at the inn to return what had been lent us in the way of baskets, pitchers, etc., a lady drove up in a stylish phaeton, and, excusing herself for intruding, said that a coach was so rarely seen in those parts she could not resist asking who we were and whither bound. I gave her all desired information, and asked her to please gratify our ladies by telling in return who she was. "Lady Stuart Monteith," was the reply. She was of the Monteiths of Closeburn Castle, as we learned from Mr. Murray, our landlord at Cumnock. The estate will go at her death to a nephew who is farming in America. We thought there must be some good reason why he did not return and manage for his aunt, who indeed seems well qualified to manage for herself. The young exiled heir had our sympathy, but long may it be ere he enters upon Closeburn, for we were all heartily in favor of a long and happy reign to the present ruler of that beautiful estate. Lady Monteith assured us that we would be well taken care of at the Dumfries Arms, and she was right. Mr. Murray and his handsome sisters will long be remembered as model hotel-keepers. They made our stay most agreeable. Mr. Murray took us to the Bowling Green in the evening, and many of our party saw the game for the first time. Great excitement prevails when the sides are evenly matched. It is like the curling pond, a perfect republic. There is no rank upon the ice or upon the green. The postman will berate the provost for bad play at bowls, but touch his hat respectfully to him on the pavement. A man may be even a provost and yet not up to giving them a "Yankee" when called for. We were curious to know what a "Yankee" shot was, for we heard it called for by the captains every now and then. We were told that this was a shot which "knocked all before it, and played the very deevil." That is not bad.

While a few of us who had recently seen the land of Burns remained at Cumnock, the remainder of the party drove to Ayr and saw all the sights there and returned in the evening. Our walks about Cumnock were delightful, and we left Mr. Murray's care with sincere regret. Mr. Wilson was upon his native heath here and did all he could to make our stay pleasant.

OLD CUMNOCK, July 19.

Passing out of the town this morning, we stopped at the prettiest little photographic establishment we had ever seen, and the artist succeeded in taking excellent views of the coach and party. It was done in an instant; we were taken ere we were aware. A great thing, that new process; one has not time to look his very worst, as sitters usually contrive to do, ladies especially.

"Right, Perry!" and off we drove through the crowd for Douglas. The general manager soon confided to me that for the first time he was dubious about our resting-place. A telegram had been received by him from the landlord at Douglas just before starting, stating that his inn was full to overflowing with officers of the volunteer regiment encamped there, and that it was simply impossible for him to provide for our party. What was to be done? It was decided to inform that important personage, mine host, that we were moving upon him, and that if he gave no quarters we should give none either. He must billet us somewhere; if not, then

> "A night in Greenwood spent
> Were but to-morrow's merriment."

But we felt quite sure that the town of Douglas would in council assembled extend a warm welcome to the Americans and see us safely housed, even if there was not a hotel in the place. So on we went. While passing through Lugar, a pretty young miss ran out of the telegraph office, and holding up both hands, called: "Stop! It's no aff yet! it's no aff yet!" A message was coming for the coaching party. It proved to be from our Douglas landlord, saying, All right! he would do the best he could for us. When the party was informed how much we had been trusting in providence for the past few hours, such was their enthusiasm that some disappointment was expressed at the assuring character of the telegram. To not know where we were going to be all night—maybe to have to lie in and on the coach—would have been such fun! "But behind yon hill where Lugar flows," sung by Eliza, sounded none the less sweet when we knew we were not likely to have to camp out upon its pretty banks. It is essential for successful happy coaching with ladies that every comfort should be provided. I am satisfied it would never do to risk the weaker sex coaching in any other land. The extreme comfort of everything here alone keeps them well and able to stand the gypsy life. We travelled most of the day through the ore lands and among the blast furnaces of the Scotch pig-iron kings, the Bairds. It is not so many years since I raised a laugh at Mr. Whitelaw's table in London by predicting that the Carnegies might some day make as much of this necessity of life as they did. In those bygone days none seemed to understand the vast resources of America, or to believe in her manifest destiny; but Mr. Whitelaw, then M. P. for Glasgow, and one of the Bairds, was one who knew the possibilities of that future better than his guests who laughed. We are ready to challenge them for a year's run any time now, and we shall beat them next year, sure.

To reach Edinburgh we had to drive diagonally eastward across the country, for we had gone to the westward that Dumfries and the Land of Burns might not be missed. This route took us through less frequented localities, off the main lines of travel, but our experience justified us in feeling that this had proved a great advantage, for we saw more of Scotland than we should have done otherwise.

Our luncheon to-day was a novel one in some respects. No inn was to be reached upon the moors, and feed for the horses had to be taken with us from Cumnock; but we found the prettiest little wimpling burn, across which a passage was made by throwing in big stones, for the shady dell was upon the far side. The horses were unhitched and allowed to nibble the wayside grass beside our big coach, which loomed up on the moor as if it were double its true size.

The thistle and the harebell begin to deck our grassy tables at noon, and fine fields of peas and beans scent the air. All is Scotch; and oh, that bracing breeze, which cools deliciously the sun's bright rays, confirms us in the opinion that no weather is like Scotch weather, when it is good; when it is not I have no doubt the same opinion is equally correct, but we have no means of judging. Scotland smiles upon her guests, and we love her with true devotion in return. "What do you think of Scotland noo?" came often to-day; but words cannot express what we do think of her. In the language of one of our young ladies, "She is just lovely."

The question came up to-day at luncheon, would one ever tire of this gypsy life? and it was unanimously voted, never! At least no one could venture to name a time when he would be ready to return to the prosy routine of ordinary existence while we had such weather and such company. Indeed, this nomadic life must be the hardest of all to exchange for city life. It is so diametrically opposed to it in every phase. "If I were not the independent gentleman I am," says Lamb, "I should choose to be a beggar." "Chapsey me a gypsy," gentle Elia, you could not have known of that life, or perhaps you considered it and the beggar's life identical. But, mark you, there is a difference which is much more than a distinction. A gypsy cannot beg, but he or she tells fortunes, tinkers a little, and deals in horses. Even if he steals a little now and then, I take it he is still within the lines of the profession, while your beggar who does anything in the way of work, or who steals, is no true man. His license is for begging only. The gypsy obviously has the wider range, and I say again therefore, "Chapsey me a gypsy," gentle Elia.

We reached pretty Douglas in the evening, and sounded our horn more than usual to apprise mine host that the host was upon him. We were greatly pleased to see him and his good wife standing in the door of the inn with pleasant, smiling faces to greet us. They had arranged everything for our comfort. Many thanks to those gentlemanly officers who had so kindly given up their rooms to accommodate their American cousins. Quarters for the gentlemen had been found in the village, and Joe and Perry and the horses were all well taken care of. Thus we successfully passed through the only occasion where there seemed to be the slightest difficulty about our resting-place for the night.

Douglas is really worth a visit. There lie many generations of the members of that family so noted in Scotland's history. Home Castle, their residence, is a commanding pile seen for many miles up the valley as we approach the town. Our visit to it was greatly enjoyed, such a pretty walk in the evening.

DOUGLAS, July 20.

Edinburgh, Scotia's darling seat, only forty-four miles distant. All aboard, this pretty morning, for Edinburgh! "Right, Perry!" and off we went quite early through Douglas, for the capital. Our path was through woods for several miles, and we listened to the birds and saw and heard many of the incidents of morn so prettily described by Beattie:

> "The wild brook babbling down the mountain-side,
> The lowing herd ; the sheep-fold's simple bell ;
> The hum of bees, and linnet's lay of love,
> And the full choir that wakes the universal grove."

It was to be a long day's drive, but an easy one ; only one hill, and then a gradual descent all the way to Edinburgh. So it might have been by the other road, but the milestones which told us so many miles to Edinburgh should also have said : "Take the new road ; this is the old one, over the hills and far away." But they did not, and we could not be wrong, for this was a way if not *the* way to "Auld Reekie." After all it was one of the richest of our experiences as we look back upon it now. So many hills to walk up and so many to walk down ; so many moors with not a house to be seen, nothing but sheep around us and the lights and shadows of a Scotch sky overhead. But it was grand, and recalled some of Black's wonderful pen pictures. And then we enjoyed the heather which we found in its beauty, though scarcely yet tinted with its richest glow of color.

About luncheon time we began to look longingly for the inn which we expected to find, but there was no habitation of any kind to be seen, and we began to suspect that, notwithstanding the milestones, which stood up and told us the lie which was half the truth (ever the blacker lie), we were not upon the right road to Edinburgh. At this juncture we met a shepherd with his collies, and learnt from him that we were still twelve miles from an inn. It was a cool, breezy day; the air had the "nip" in it which Maggie missed so in England, and we were famishing. There was nothing else to do but to stop where we were, at the pretty burn, and tarry there for entertainment for man and beast.

As proof of our temperance, please note that the flasks filled with sherry, whiskey, and brandy, at Brighton I believe, as reserve forces for emergencies, still had plenty in them when called for to-day; and rarely has a glass of spirits done greater good, the ladies as well as we of the stronger sex feeling that a glass was necessary to keep off a chill. We were "o'er the moors among the heather" in good earnest to-day, but how soon we were all set to rights and laughing over our frolic. The shepherd and his dogs lunched with us, and many a glint of Scottish shepherd life did we get from his conversation. He was a happy, contented man, and ever so grateful that he was not condemned to live in a city. He thought such a cramped-up life would soon kill him.

Good-bye, my gentle shepherd and "Tweed" and "Rab," your faithful, sagacious companions.

Your life leads to contentment, and where will you find that jewel when you leave mother earth and her products, her heather and her burns, your doggies and your sheep?

Davie, in Andrew Martin's absence, sang us that song whose prettiest verse, though they are all fine, is this:

> "See yonder paukie shepherd
> Wha lingers on the hill,
> His ewes are in the fauld
> And his sheep are lying still."

Softly, softly, pianissimo, my boy! These lines must be sung so, not loudly like the other verses. Andrew knows the touch.

> "But he downa gang to rest,
> For his heart is in a flame
> To meet his bonnie lassie,
> When the kye come hame."

And so we parted from our shepherd, the chorus of our song reaching him over the moors till he faded out of sight. I am sure we wish him weel. Happiness is not all, nor mainly, in the higher walks of life; and surely in virtue's paths the cottage leaves the palace far behind.

Another song followed, which I thought equally appropriate, for it tells us that "Ilka blade o' grass keps its ain drap o' dew." Ah, the shepherd's drops of the dew of life are often something that princes sigh for in vain.

After many miles up and down, we finally reached the top of a hill from which we saw lying before us, though still fourteen miles distant, the modern Athens. There was no mistaking Arthur's Seat, the lion crouching there. "Stop, Perry!" Three times three for the "Queen of the Unconquered North!" "What do you think of Scotland noo?" Match that city who can! Not on this planet will you do it, search where you may.

It was only a few miles from where we now stood that Fitz Eustace, enraptured with the scene,

> "And making demi-volte in air,
> Cried, Where's the coward that would not dare
> To fight for such a land!"

Fight for it? I guess so, to the death! Scotland forever!

We were about completing one stage of our journey, for Edinburgh had been looked forward to as one of the principal points we had to reach, and we were to rest there a few days before marching upon the more ancient metropolis, Dunfermline. Most of us had been steadily at work since we left Brighton, and the prospect of a few days' respite was an agreeable one; but after all it was surprising how fresh even the ladies were.

Miss Roxburgh was here called to the front, alongside of Perry, to act as guide into and through the city to our hotel in Prince's Street. The enthusiasm grew more and more intense as we came nearer and fresh views were obtained. There remained one more tollgate, one of the few which have not yet been abolished. Joe had as usual gone forward to pay the toll, but the keeper declared she did not know the charge, as never since she kept toll had anything like that—pointing to the coach—passed there. Was it any wonder that we attracted attention during our progress northward?

From one hill-top I caught a sight of the sparkling Forth, and beyond where lay "the dearest spot on earth to me." The town could not be seen, but when I was able to cry, "Dunfermline lies there," three rousing cheers were given for the "Auld gray Toon."

EDINBURGH, July 21–26.

Our route lay through Newington, that we might leave the young artist at home. We tried to do it quietly, but our friend Mrs. Hill was out and shaking hands with us ere we could drive off. Mr. MacGregor of the Royal had been mindful of us; a grand sitting-room fronting on Prince's Street and overlooking the gardens gave us the best possible view, the very choice spot of all this choice city. The night was beautiful, and the lights from the towering houses of the old town made an illumination as it were in honor of our arrival. That the travellers were delighted with Edinburgh, that it more than fulfilled all expectations, is to say but little; and those who saw it for the first time felt it to be beyond all that they had imagined. Those of us who knew its picturesque charms were more than ever impressed with its superiority over all other cities. Take my word for it, my readers, there is no habitation of human beings in this world as fine in its way, and its way itself is fine, as this the capital of Scotland.

The surprise and delight of my friends gave me much pleasure. Scotland had already won all hearts. They had admired England, but they loved Scotland. Ah, how could they help it! I loved her too more deeply than ever.

It is best to disband a large party when in a city possessed of many and varied attractions, allowing each little group to see the sights in its own way; assembling, however, at breakfast and dinner, and spending the evenings together, recounting the day's adventures. This was the general order issued for Edinburgh.

Mother and Miss Franks were the guests of Mrs. D. O. Hill, a Dunfermline bairn of whom we are all proud (a woman who does man's work in marble is something to be proud of); so that our hotel party was something of a republic in the absence of the Queen Dowager.

The new docks at Leith were opened with much ceremony during our stay, and I took a party of our Edinburgh friends upon the coach to witness the opening. It was not a clear day, meteorologically considered, but nevertheless it was a happy one for the coaching party. Upon our return, a stop at Mr. Nelson's magnificent residence was specially agreeable. He and his daughters were most kind to us while in Edinburgh. Mr. Nelson gave us a rare treat by showing us through their immense printing establishment, where such exquisite things are done, such Easter and Christmas cards, such friendship tokens, and a thousand other lovely forms we had never seen before in their various stages of manufacture.

I asked Mr. Nelson what he had to say in reply to the admissions of the leading art authorities of the superiority of American work in black and white, such as our magazines excel in. He said this could not be questioned; there was nothing done in British publications that equalled the American. The reason he gave furnishes food for thought. I pray you, fellow countrymen, take note of it. Two principal American illustrated magazines, *Harper's* and the *Century*, print each more than one hundred thousand copies, while no British magazine prints half that number. The American publisher can consequently afford to pay twice as much as the British publisher for his illustrations. If this be the true reason of America's superiority in this respect, and I am sure Mr. Nelson knows what he is stating, then as its population increases more rapidly than the British the difference between their respective publications must increase, and finally drive the home article into a very restricted position. Pursuing this fact to its logical conclusion, Britain may soon receive from her giant child all that is best in any department of art which depends upon general support for success. This seems to me to betoken a revolution, not as implying the inherent superiority of the American, but simply flowing from the fact that fifty millions of English-speaking and reading people can afford to spend more for any certain article than thirty-five millions can. That Colonel Mapleson now brings over Her Majesty's Opera Company for the New York season as regularly as he opens his London season, and especially that he makes far more profit out of the former than out of the latter, is another significant fact. That leading actors find a wider field here than at home is still another, and even ministers are finding that the call of the Lord to higher labors and higher salaries often comes from the far side of the Atlantic. Drs. McCosh, Hall,

Ormiston, and Taylor, our leading divines, get treble salaries in the Republic, and are said to be valuable importations. As Mr. Evarts said one night in a post-prandial effort: "They are about the only specimens of 'the cloth' which is admitted duty free." As long as America sent Britain only pork and cheese and provisions, and such products of the soil, it was all well enough, but if she is beginning to send the highest things of life, the art treasures, which give sweetness and light to human existence, it is somewhat alarming. For my part, I do not like to think that these Americans are to send Britain every good thing, and that the once proud country that led the world is to stand receiving as it were the crumbs from this rich land's table. In one department America can be kept second for as long a term as we need trouble about—she has nothing to compare with the leading English Reviews. Our generation will see no close rival to the *Fortnightly* or the *Nineteenth Century*, to *Blackwood* or *Chambers's Journal*, or to the *Edinburgh* or *Westminster Review*; although the *North American* and the *International* show that even in this race America enters two not indifferent steeds.

I must not forget to mention that the birds in the *Century* magazine which the *Athenæum* pronounced so far superior to any British work were designed by a young lady and engraved by her sister. The work of two American young ladies excelled the best of England; and then did not Miss Rosina Emmet send a Christmas greeting of her own composition to friends in England which took the second prize at the London Exhibition, although not intended for anything more than a private token of friendship. Let a note be made of all this, with three loving cheers for the young lady artists of the Republic. Instead of losing the charms of women by giving public expression to their love of the beautiful in all its forms, they but add one more indescribable charm which their less fortunate sisters can never hope to attain. How a man does reverence a woman who does fine things in art, literature, or music, or in any line whatever!

The Charioteers gave leave of absence to the chief and general manager to spend Sunday with my friends Mr. and Mrs. Glover, at Strathairly House, on the banks of the Forth. It was a most delightful visit. The Commodore of the Forth Yachting Squadron (for such friend Glover is) had the Ranee ready to take us back to Edinburgh Monday morning. We enjoyed the sail down the Forth very much. That we could not accept the Commodore's invitation to change the Gay Charioteers into the Bold Mariners for a day and visit St. Andrews in the Ranee gave rise to deep regret, when the other members of the party were informed of the treat proposed; but we cannot glean every field upon our march. Some other time, Commodore, the recently elected member of the squadron will report for duty on the flagship and splice the main-brace with you and your jolly crew.

Upon our return to Edinburgh Monday morning, the first rumbling of the distant thunder from Dunfermline was heard, and it dawned upon us that serious work was at hand. Our friend, Mr. Donald of the Council, had called upon us and intimated that

something of a demonstration might be made upon
our arrival in the native town ; but when I found a
telegram from Mr. Simpson, the clerk, asking us to
postpone our coming for a day, I knew there was an
end to play. Things looked serious, but I was not
going to be the sole sufferer. At dinner I laid it down
as the law from which there could be no appeal, that
if there was any public speaking to be done, Messrs.
Phipps, McCargo, King, McCandless, and Vandevort, in the order named, were in for it. It is surprising how much it mitigates one's own troubles to
see his dearest friends more frightened than himself. I grew bolder as I encouraged these victims.
The last two offered great inducements to the ladies
if they would vote that they should be excused. As
for the others, I made it a question of ministerial
confidence, and the administration was sustained.
When you read their speeches I am sure you will see
the wisdom of my selections.

Tuesday was rainy, but with luncheon at Mr.
Rose's (which we should have been so sorry to miss,
for we had known Miss Rose of old as one of Emma's
most cherished friends), and a party in the evening
at Mrs. Hill's, the day was a busy one.

I was glad to see Sir Noel Paton, Dunfermline's
most distinguished son, able to be at his sister's that
evening. The recent narrow and heroic escape from
drowning of himself, Lady Paton, and his son Victor, gave us all renewed interest in grasping his hand
again. Thrown from a small sail-boat into the sea,
at least two hundred yards from shore, with ropes
and sail tangled about them, the three rallied to each
other's support (for all could swim), and bore each

other up until finally Lady Paton got between her husband and son, with one hand on the shoulder of each, and thus they struggled grandly to shore. Where is another trio that could do that, think you? I tell you who don't know Dunfermline, that these Patons were always a marked family, and have had genius hovering about their pretty home for generations, and now and then touching the heads and hearts of father, sons, and daughters with its creative wand. There is a great deal in blood, no doubt, but the blood from an honest weaver or shoemaker is, as a rule, a much better article, something to be much prouder of, than you find from nobles whose rise came from such conduct as should make their descendants ashamed to talk of descent. It's a God's mercy we are all from honest weavers; let us pity those who haven't ancestors of whom they can be proud, dukes or duchesses though they be.

DUNFERMLINE, July 27-28.

Put all the fifty days of our journey together, and we would have exchanged them all for rainy ones if we could have been assured a bright day for this occasion. It came, a magnificent day. The sun shone forth as if glad to shine upon this the most memorable day of my mother's life or of mine, as far as days can be rendered memorable by the actions of our fellowmen. We left Edinburgh and reached Queensferry in time for the noon boat. Here was the scene so finely given in "Marmion," which I tried, however, in vain to recall as I gazed upon it. If Dunfermline and its thunders had not been in the distance, I think

I could have given it after a fashion, but I failed altogether that morning.

> "But northward far, with purer blaze,
> On Ochil mountains fell the rays,
> And as each heathy top they kissed,
> It gleamed a purple amethyst.
> Yonder the shores of Fife you saw;
> Here Preston Bay, and Berwick Law;
> And broad between them rolled,
> The gallant Firth the eye might note,
> Whose islands on its bosom float,
> Like emeralds chased in gold."

And truly it was a morning in which nature's jewels sparkled at their best. Upon reaching the north shore we were warmly greeted by Uncle and Aunt Lauder, and Maggie and Annie. It was decided better not to risk luncheon in the ruins of Rosythe Castle, as we had intended, the grass being reported damp from recent rains. We accordingly drove to the inn, but we were met at the door by the good landlady, who, with uplifted hands, exclaimed: "I'm a' alane! There's naebody in the house! They're a' awa' to Dunfermline! There'll be great goings on there the day."

A hotel without one servant. The good woman, however, assured us we might come in and help ourselves to anything in the house; so we managed to enjoy our luncheon, some of us only after a fashion. There were three gentlemen, a wife, and a cousin who for the first time did not care much for anything in the form of luncheon. Speeches, speeches, these are what troubled Harry, Davie, and me; and I had cause for grave alarm, of which they could form little idea, for I felt that if Dunfermline had been touched and her people had determined to give us a public reception, there was no saying to what lengths they might go.

If I could decently have stolen away and gone round by some circuitous route, sending my fellow townsmen an apology, and telling them that I really felt myself unable to undergo the ordeal, I should have been tempted to do so. I was also afraid that mother would break down, for if ever her big black eyes get wet it's all over with her. How fortunate it was that Mrs. Hill was with her to keep her right! It was wisely resolved that she should take mother inside of the coach and watch over her. I bit my lip, told the Charioteers they were in for it and must go through without flinching, that now the crisis had come I was just bound to stand anything. I was past stage-fright, and I assured myself that they could do their worst—I was callous and would not be moved—but to play the part of a popular hero even for a day, wondering all the time what you have done to deserve the outburst, is fearful work. When I did get time to think of it, my tower of strength lay in the knowledge that the spark which had set fire to their hearts was mother's return and her share in the day's proceedings. Grand woman, she has deserved all that was done in her honor even on that day. What she has done for her two boys is incredible—a romance if truly written—but what she has done for herself is more incredible still, for she is the centre from which radiates, in small as in great things, the clear rays of unimpeachable truth and honor. Mother's statements, from " I shall be glad to see you," uttered to an acquaintance, up to the most serious things of life, fall as if preceded with "thus saith the Lord," for they are always true. So I kept myself strong in the knowledge that this ovation was for her, and stronger in the further faith that it was deserved.

A man stopped us at the junction of the roads to inform us that we were expected to pass through the ancient borough of Innerkeithing, but I forgot myself there. It seemed a fair chance to escape part of the excitement (we had not yet begun the campaign as it were) ; at all events I dodged, to escape the first fire, as raw troops are always said to do, and so we took the direct road. When the top of the Ferry Hills was reached we saw the town, all as dead as if the holy Sabbath lay upon it, without one evidence of life. How beautiful is Dunfermline seen from the Ferry Hills, its grand old abbey towering over all, seeming to hallow the city and to lend a charm and dignity to the lowliest tenement. Nor is there in all broad Scotland, nor in many places elsewhere that I know of, a more varied and delightful view than that obtained from the park upon a fine day. What Benares is to the Hindoo, Mecca to the Mohammedan, Jerusalem to the Christian, all that Dunfermline is to me.

But here I must stop. If you want to learn how impulsive and enthusiastic the Scotch are when once aroused, how dark and stern and true is the North, and yet how fervid and overwhelming in its love when the blood is up, I do not know where you will find a better evidence of it than in what follows. See how small a spark kindled so great a flame. Mother and I are still somewhat shamefaced about it, but somehow or other we managed to go through with our parts without breaking down.

DUNFERMLINE, July 27-28.

The following are the accounts, from the *Press* and *Journal* newspapers of Dunfermline, of July 30, 1881, which seem necessary to make the record of the trip complete, but which all except those deeply interested may skip:

THE CARNEGIE DEMONSTRATION.

There was one feature in the great demonstration which took place in Dunfermline on Wednesday, that must have very much enhanced its value in the eyes of the public-spirited gentleman in whose honor it was held, and that was, its almost entire unanimity. There may have been some difference of opinion at first among the inhabitants as to the advisability of adopting the Libraries Act in Dunfermline, as there was lately in Edinburgh; but there did not seem to be any at all either as to the value of the gifts which Mr. Andrew Carnegie has bestowed upon his native town, or as to the propriety of doing all due honor to the man to whom honor was due. If all the inhabitants of Dunfermline did not take part in the magnificent procession which took place, few there were who did not turn out to the Public Park or the streets to do full justice to the occasion. Great as are the benefits which Mr. Carnegie has bestowed upon Dunfermline, and much as these are appreciated by the inhabitants, it may safely be said, however, that the enthusiasm which was manifested at the laying of the memorial stone of the Free Library on Wednesday had a deeper significance than the mere gratitude which most people naturally feel for favors received. Mr. Carnegie is, in every sense of the word, a representative man; and all classes of the community recognize in him an example of self-reliance, energy, perseverance, and generous-heartedness, that not only do honor to the "Auld Gray Toon," but may prove an incentive in the future to generations yet unborn. It was in this spirit, we doubt not, that so many trades, public works, societies, and fraternities combined to do honor to their former townsman; and, certainly, no more stirring sight was ever seen in Dunfermline than when the people, assembled in their thousands in the Public Park, gave him a right hearty welcome to his native town, and, in well-chosen words, expressed their gratitude to him for the invaluable gifts which he had bestowed upon the community. The American friends who are travelling with Mr. Carnegie and his revered mother have seen a good many demonstrations in their day—even the great demonstration at Leith on Tuesday, on the opening of the new Edinburgh dock—and have themselves received much respect and consideration while on their "four-in-hand" journey through England to Scotland; but they have had to confess, that they were more than surprised at the spontaneous burst of enthusiasm with which Mr. Carnegie and his respected mother were everywhere received in Dunfermline. It was a revelation to them which they will not soon forget; and however much they may have been disposed to believe in the familiar adage, "Out of sight, out of mind," they were compelled to admit that to whatever part of the world the sons of Dunfermline may wander to fight out for themselves "the battle of life," and to whatever position they may attain in the struggle, they are still remembered with kindly feelings by the "old folks at home," and are gladly welcomed by all who know them when they return to the scenes of their youth. Perhaps there was no more affecting part of Wednesday's proceedings than when the successful man of business—the wealthy and influential iron king of Pittsburgh and New York—paused, in his triumphant progress through the town, at the humble dwelling where he was born, and took a long and loving look at the plain old building; or when, in the evening at the great banquet which was held in St. Margaret's Hall, the large and influential assembly joined heartily in the refrain of the fine old Scotch ballad, "Will ye no' come back again"—a refrain, it need hardly be said, which was most appropriate to the occasion, and which produced upon Mr. Carnegie and his lady and gentlemen friends an effect that was as touching as it was creditable to them.

But much as Dunfermline has to thank Mr. Carnegie for, she is by no means the only recipient of his bounties. It was only the other day that an institute not a hundred miles from Bannockburn had to acknowledge his generosity in the form of a large subscription which he had presented to it, in aid of the commendable objects it has in view. And we have it from the best authority, that it is one of the standing rules in the office of his great establishment in New York, that no native of Dunfermline who calls upon him for advice or assistance is ever to be sent away without his knowledge or without seeing him if at all possible. Like most great business men who have carved out a fortune for themselves by their own indomitable energy and intellectual ability, Mr. Carnegie is liable to be dropped upon by impostors; but we believe that no real case of hardship or of difficulty has ever come before him personally without his having done something to the removal of it. In one word, in doing honor to Mr. Carnegie and his personal friends on Wednesday, the people of Dunfermline did honor to one whose deeds of charity and benevolence are as well, and perhaps better, known in the country of his adoption than they are in his native town. And we can only re-echo the sentiments which were expressed by so many influential gentlemen at the banquet in the evening— that the Public Baths and the Free Library which Mr. Carnegie has so generously presented to the town will be taken advantage of in such a way as will show him that their real worth are duly appreciated by the community whose welfare he has so deeply at heart.

MR. CARNEGIE'S "FOUR-IN-HAND" TOUR.

The interesting journey which Mr. Carnegie is now making through Scotland, as he has already done in England, will give the American friends who accompany him a good opportunity of carrying away with them many pleasant memories of the "old country." The mode of travelling which he has adopted is one which brings to mind the old coaching days, with the exciting vicissitudes of the road, the quaint but picturesque villages and old hostelries, and the broad expanse of landscape and ever-changing scenes which meet the eye from the comfortable outside seat of a well-appointed "four-in-hand," as it bowls along. And when Mr. Carnegie contemplated so lengthened a journey as he is now making, he did well, we think, in arranging to travel in the old-fashioned style, and to carry along with him the necessary materials and appliances for ministering to the creature comforts of himself and numerous party. His journey has as yet proved a very pleasant and agreeable one ; and Dunfermline is not the only town which he has passed through that has received him with marked honor and respect ; nor is the silver trowel which was presented to Mrs. Carnegie after she laid the memorial stone of the Dunfermline Free Library the only presentation that has been made during the course of the journey. Starting from Brighton, shortly after their arrival from America, Mr. Carnegie and his mother, along with their American and other friends, proceeded through various parts of England on their way to Scotland. His party included Mr. and Mrs. King, and Mr. G. F. McCandless, of New York ; Mr. and Mrs. McCargo, Miss J. Johns, Mr. H. Phipps, Jr., and Mr. B. F. Vandevort, of Pittsburgh ; Miss Alice French, Davenport ; and Miss Emma Franks, Liverpool. Among other places which they visited was Windsor, where Mrs. Carnegie was presented by the party with a handsome gold-plated silver cup on reaching her seventy-first birthday. From Windsor, the party visited in succession Oxford, Warwick Castle, Kenilworth, Coventry, Birmingham, and Wolverhampton—at the latter of which places they were hospitably entertained for a week by Mr. and

Mrs. T. Graham (late Mrs. Whitelaw, Dunfermline), and many other friends. Lichfield, Dovedale, and Kendal were next passed through; and on the arrival of the party at the Westmoreland Lakes, a halt was called, and a pleasant week was spent in visiting the beautiful scenes which the poet Wordsworth has immortalized by his pen. Proceeding next to Dumfries, the party were kindly entertained by Mr. Nelson, of Friars Carse (Ellisland), where Mr. and Mrs. Carnegie renewed their recollections of our national poet, " Robert Burns." Arrived at Lanark, an interesting visit was made to Douglas Castle; then posting on to Edinburgh—where the more prominent objects of interest in the metropolis of Scotland were inspected—some of the party proceeded to Leith on Tuesday to witness the great demonstration at the opening of the new Edinburgh dock. The visit to Dunfermline—the most interesting and most memorable of all—is fully described elsewhere; and yesterday forenoon Mr. Carnegie and party set off in their " four-in-hand " for a tour to the north of Scotland, by way of Perth and Dunkeld. Among those who have already accompanied Mr. Carnegie and his American friends during a portion of their journey may be mentioned Mr. and Mrs. Graham, Wolverhampton; Miss Jane Reid, the Misses Lauder, Miss K. Graham, and Mr. A. Martin, Dunfermline—all of whom, we need hardly say, can testify to the geniality and hospitality of their entertainer, the harmony and good humor that prevailed among the company, and the healthful enjoyment which all experienced in their rather unusual but delightful mode of travelling.

LAYING OF THE MEMORIAL STONE OF THE CARNEGIE FREE LIBRARY.

GREAT DEMONSTRATION.

The memorial stone of the Carnegie Free Library was laid on Wednesday by Mrs. Carnegie, the mother of the generous donor, amid great enthusiasm. Seldom if ever has Dunfermline witnessed such a grand display of flags and banners, or the organization of a procession so large in numbers, so orderly, so enthusiastic, and so picturesque in appearance. Every one in the community seemed to vie with each other in making the occasion memorable, and the result was a decided success, far exceeding the most sanguine anticipations regarding it. The demonstration may be said to be unparalleled in the history of Dunfermline, and was alike worthy of the gentleman in whose honor it was made and the occasion which called it forth.

It falls to the lot of very few towns to have such a son as Mr. Carnegie, who amid all the worldly wealth which he has so honorably amassed for himself in a foreign land, still evinces a deep and keen interest in the welfare of his native city of Dunfermline, and exhibits that interest in generously providing it with public baths and a free library—gifts calculated to be of immense benefit to the inhabitants. It was therefore only proper, when Mr. Carnegie, who is accompanied by Mrs. Carnegie and a number of friends from America, expressed his intention of visiting Dunfermline for the purpose of having the memorial stone laid of the institution which he has so handsomely gifted to the town, that business should be generally suspended, and the inhabitants turn out and give him a hearty reception, as a token of the gratitude they entertain for the great benefits he has bestowed upon his native town. The manner in which this was done on Wednesday showed very unmistakably how much the inhabitants of Dunfermline appreciate his generosity. The idea of having a demonstration worthy of the occasion was first mooted by the Library Committee, who respectfully invited the different trades and public bodies to meet and make the necessary arrangements. The representatives of these bodies entered enthusiastically into the matter, and the arrangements made were of a very satisfactory character, and were carried into effect most successfully.

THE DECORATIONS THROUGHOUT THE TOWN.

From an early hour on Wednesday great preparations were made to give the town a gay appearance, and the efforts of a large number of people to do so with suitable decorations had the desired effect. From private and public buildings numerous flags and banners were displayed; and on the Corporation Buildings there floated the Scottish Standard and a flag bearing the city arms. At other points in the High Street bunting was exhibited— the strings of flags from Mr. R. Nicol junior's shop across to the Townhouse, and to the roof of the old library building, especially, being very effective; but what attracted the most attention was a huge banner hung across the street from Mr. Rolland's shop, which bore the very appropriate motto, " Welcome Carnegie, generous son." Farther along the street a line of flags was stretched across from Mr. Taylor's studio to Mr. Grieve's shop, on which was the word, "Trinacria." On the Gate Tower of the palace were floating the national flags of America, England, and Scotland. Here due honor was done to the combined flags by Mr. Carnegie's carriage stopping underneath them, and the occupants giving vent to their patriotic feelings in several rounds of cheers. At St. Margaret's Hall, the Post-Office, the City Arms and other hotels, the Music Hall, banks, shops, factories, and other public works, there was more or less bunting displayed; while at the entrance of the town at Bothwell Street was erected a very tasteful triumphal arch. The greatest display, however, was at the Library Buildings, which were decorated in a very artistic manner.

THE PROCESSION.

To the general public the most attractive feature of the day's proceedings was the large and picturesque procession. Work was generally suspended at one o'clock, and the streets from that time wore a very lively aspect. Crowds of people were to be seen taking advantage of the most prominent places from which a good view could be obtained of the pageant. The arrangements made were closely adhered to in all details, and at three o'clock large contingents from the various trades, public works, and societies, wended their way to the Public Park, which was the general marshalling ground of the procession. Here a great crowd of people had assembled on the slopes above the central walk, and the movements of the marshals—Messrs. Robertson,

Halliday, and Sergeant Brown—as they proceeded to arrange the procession in proper order, were watched with much interest. At half-past three o'clock, the time appointed for the procession to start, every one of the different works and societies were in their allotted places, and, accompanied by the Elgin, Townhill, Lassodie, Crossgates, and Fordell brass bands, who were placed at intervals, the procession moved off, amid great cheering, in the following order: Oddfellows, Dyers, Bakers; Free Gardeners, including the Ancient Society; Foresters, workers at Dunfermline Foundry; the work people at Victoria and Castleblair, Canmore, St. Leonard's, Dunfermline, Caledonian, St. Margaret's, Abbey Gardens, Bothwell, Albany, and Clayacres Factories, including Bleachers. The route taken was by Comely Park Place and New Row. The procession presented a very imposing appearance, and numbered about 8000—5000 of which may be safely said to have represented the different factories. The spectacle which the procession presented as they proceeded to Bothwell Street was one which is seldom witnessed. The clean and tidy appearance of the females and the other workers in the factories—many of whom bore flags, with suitable mottoes, and various miniature designs of the machines used in the preparation and weaving of the damask linen; the lively costumes of the Oddfellows, Gardeners, and Foresters, with the peculiar insignia of their order and other emblems of brotherhood, along with the display of the Dyers, Bakers, and Bleachers, made a pageant which all who witnessed it or took part in it will long remember. The head of the procession reached

Bothwell Place shortly before four o'clock, and here the Provost, Magistrates, and Town Council were stationed at each side of the street in brakes, in which they had been driven down from the Townhouse, preceded by three pipers and the burgh officer with his halberd. A large concourse of people had assembled here to give Mr. Carnegie a hearty welcome on his approach to the town. Punctual to time— four o'clock—Mr. Carnegie, along with a party of friends, drove up in his four-in-hand coach, and the crowd received him with loud and prolonged cheering, which Mr. Carnegie gracefully acknowledged. Shortly after, the processionists began to move, and as they passed the Gusset House, constant and hearty cheers were given by them—the females waving their handkerchiefs. The procession took fully twenty minutes to pass, and was upward of a mile in length. The distinguished visitors, with the members of the Town Council, followed the procession; and as they were driven through the crowded streets, Mr. Carnegie received a perfect ovation from the people, which he repeatedly acknowledged. The route taken was by the Netherton and Moodie Street. As soon as the top of this street was reached the carriages were stopped opposite the house in which Mr. Carnegie was born, which is on the east side of the street. Hearty cheers were at once raised by the strangers and crowd, after which the party proceeded up Gibb Street, Monastery Street, Kirkgate, High Street, East Port Street, and Holyrood Place—Mr. Carnegie meantime receiving enthusiastic greetings from the occupants of the well-filled windows and the people on the different streets, and the bells of the Abbey and Townhouse ringing out merry peals all the while. The three carriages passed through an assemblage of people, who must have numbered 10,000, to a platform which had been erected on the south side of the upper walk to enable the workingmen to present Mr. Carnegie with an

ILLUMINATED ADDRESS.

As soon as the platform was filled, the people crowded round it as close as possible in order to witness the proceedings. The company on the platform included Mrs. and Mr. Carnegie ; Mrs. D. O. Hill, Edinburgh ; Mr. Carnegie's friends ; ex-Provost Mathieson ; Provost Walls ; Bailies Walker, Steedman, Seath, and Lamond ; ex-Bailie Inglis ; Treasurer Blair ; Councillors Beveridge, Donald, Alston, Lee, Brown, Roberton, Spence, and Stewart ; Messrs. J. Drummond, R. Reid, G. Lauder, G. W. Robertson, and J. C. Walker, architect, Edinburgh. The committee appointed by the workingmen to prepare and present the address were then introduced to Mr. Carnegie and Provost Walls, and immediately

Mr. D. Thomson, manager of the Abbey Garden Works, said : We, the workingmen of Dunfermline—and in speaking of the workingmen I suppose I may take in the whole city—we regard this day as one of no little importance in our annals. It is not every day that a free library is inaugurated in our midst. We believe that this institution, which is now about to be opened, will be of great credit to the city and of great value to us workingmen; and we desire, on the present occasion, to offer to the liberal donor of the Public Baths and Free Library one word at least of thanks and welcome. (Cheers.) Time was when the workingmen of Dunfermline were regarded as perhaps one of the most intelligent communities in the country, and candidates for political honors knew that they need not come here talking soft nothings, the political leavings of other communities, and with nothing but the adventitious aids of family connection; but that unless they came with sound arguments and well-hardened facts they need not come at all. I do believe to some extent we are distinguished by the same qualities of our forefathers. The weavers of a past generation or two had perhaps more liberty during the day than we have, and they could come out in mid-forenoon to read the newspapers, and discuss and heckle the characters of men in high places; but if we cannot come out of our places at mid-forenoon, or mid-afternoons, we have our evenings, and we want some means by which these evenings may be spent in a rational and intelligent manner. Our benefactor, Mr. Carnegie, in his own liberal way, has now provided that in a very handsome manner. (Cheers.) I hope that, in future years, this library will tell upon the men of Dunfermline, and that the workingmen especially, for whom these benefits are mainly directed, will take advantage of this library, and show by their attendance and appreciation how much they value such a noble institution. (Loud cheers.) Without saying more, I will now read the address which we have prepared. It is as follows:

"*Address by the Workingmen of the City of Dunfermline to Andrew Carnegie, Esq., of New York, on the occasion of the Laying of the Memorial Stone of the Carnegie Free Library,* 27 *July,* 1881.

"SIR,—We, the workingmen of Dunfermline, gladly avail ourselves of this opportunity of welcoming you to your native city, and of expressing to you our high appreciation of your noble generosity to this community.

" While rejoicing in the success which has attended your commercial enterprises, it is particularly gratifying to the sons of the ' Auld Gray Toon ' that your generous mind has found means of usefulness for part of your worldly wealth by seeking to benefit the working classes of this town.

" By your handsome gift of Public Baths and a Free Library, you have shown a real interest in our welfare, and we now desire to assure you of our heartfelt gratitude for these inestimable boons.

" It is our earnest wish that you may long be spared to enjoy continued health and happiness, and that prosperity which has hitherto attended you in the land of your adoption.

" In name and on behalf of the workingmen of Dunfermline.

    (Signed)   " PETER EASSON.
                 "   DANIEL THOMSON.
                 "   PETER BLACKWOOD.
                 "   JOHN WEIR.
                 "   JAMES BROWN."

Loud and prolonged cheers greeted the closing of the address, which was written on vellum, and executed by Messrs. Scott & Ferguson, Edinburgh ; and when Mr. Carnegie rose to reply the acclamations were again enthusiastically renewed.

Mr. Carnegie said : " Workingmen and women of Dunfermline, it seems to me at this moment as if I had been searching all my life for some great prize, I knew not what, and that it has been just laid at my feet. Nothing could so have touched my heart, nor the heart of my mother, as the spontaneous and magnificent ovation vouchsafed to us at the hands of our fellow-workmen and workingwomen of Dunfermline—(cheers)—for I tell you that I am proud to claim the title of a workingman. I am not only one who works with his brains, but one who, like yourselves, has toiled with his hands. The first dollar that I ever earned was in a manufactory, filling the spools, as many of you do this day. (Cheers.) I have come from the great Republic, where I have learned the true political gospel that labor—what a man himself does—constitutes the only true title to honor—(cheers)—and I tell you, my friends, the day is not far distant when all of you will decline to honor a man on account of his birth; and a noble man, no matter what his birth, will scorn to wear a title which he has not himself earned. (Cheers.) My friends, I have presented to you a Free Library, because I thought it the greatest blessing which it was in the power of one of yourselves to bestow upon this community. (Cheers.) Had I known a better gift to bestow upon you, my love for Dunfermline and the interest I take in all her inhabitants would have led me to bestow that gift. I am sure my mother and myself are very far from viewing this ovation, worthy of a conqueror returning in triumph, as a personal affair; we receive it as evidence that you fully appreciate the gift, and are determined to take advantage of the manifold blessings which a Free Library is calculated to bestow. (Cheers.) You may dine upon humble fare, but when you enter the portals of the Library a banquet worthy of the gods is yours; and let me tell you that you enter this Library—not as strangers, not to commune solely with men of a class above your own—but in a large measure to receive the highest wisdom from men whose hands have actually toiled as yours have done. You have Shakespeare, the mightiest of all intellects, and your own genius Burns, the ploughman. (Cheers.) My friends, we must learn never to forget that there is no title to honor to be compared with that of the day's task honestly done. (Cheers.) I will keep you no longer, but allow me to say before closing, that it is impossible that any act which I may perform in after life can give me the gratification flowing from this if you, by your free and generous use of the Library, enable me to indulge the sweet thought that it has been my privilege to bestow upon Dunfermline, my native town, a Free Library, which has proved itself a fountain of good to my fellow-townsmen." (Loud and prolonged cheers.)

This terminated the proceedings at the park; and the party, descending from the platform, entered the carriages and, amid the plaudits of the multitude, took their way to the Free Library building, where Mrs. Carnegie was to lay the memorial stone.

THE LAYING OF THE MEMORIAL STONE.

The route taken by the party to reach the Library was by East Port Street, New Row, and Canmore Street; and on arriving at Abbot Street, at half-past five o'clock, where a dense crowd had assembled to witness the interesting ceremony of laying the memorial stone of the Library, the distinguished visitors received a great ovation. The different points of vantage surrounding the Library buildings were fully occupied; and people were seen perched on the roofs of the houses opposite, while several sat on chimney-cans, in order to obtain a good view. A platform, nearly on a level with the top of the doorway where the stone was to be laid, was erected inside the buildings, to accommodate a large company of ladies and gentlemen, who were admitted by ticket. The accommodation proved to be small enough for the number that availed themselves of the privilege. After Mrs. and Mr. Carnegie, Provost Walls, and the members of the Committee had gathered in front of the stone,

Provost Walls said if there were two institutions in any city in modern days more required than others, they were a free library and public baths. Some years ago, the people of Dunfermline resolved on obtaining an additional supply of water. They had scarcely got it in when a friend from the other side of the Atlantic came to visit them, and he bethought him how he could best apply a portion of it for their benefit in some other way than through the painful means of an assessment. That friend, like a good-hearted magician, made a stroke with his wand, the Baths arose, and they were now in use. It took some time before people became sufficiently educated to be able fully to appreciate even the most useful things, but in that respect he was glad to say that the Baths were prospering every month in increased ratio, as compared with the corresponding months of previous years. A Free Library, however, was entirely different from baths. (Cheers.) Education has been going on, and people are ready for it. Formerly education was general, but now it was universal ; and, in order to enjoy the advantage of such buildings as a Free Library, people must read fluently and intelligently. That the people of Dunfermline thoroughly appreciated the erection and furnishing of such a Library was evident from what they saw before them. The hearty demonstration they had witnessed was a testimony of the gratitude of the people for the boon which had been conferred on them; and he had no doubt that generations to come would still more value its aids and avail themselves of its contents, and always bless the name of Carnegie. (Cheers.) Turning to Mrs. Carnegie, the Provost said : " I have now to address myself to you, Madam. By the magnificent generosity of your noble son we owe this valuable gift, and I have now to ask you to lay the memorial stone. When the Committee in charge of the arrangements heard that Mr. Carnegie was likely to be in Scotland, they immediately agreed to ask him to lay the memorial stone, as it was too late to lay the foundation stone. With that filial love and reverence which does him infinite honor, Mr. Carnegie replied, ' I would like you to ask my mother to do it.' (Cheers.) I have, therefore, now to ask you to lay the memorial stone of a building which will show to all generations what Mr. Carnegie has done for his native town. (Cheers.) I have now to present you with this silver trowel."

Mr. Carnegie then deposited a hermetically-sealed bottle in the cavity, which contained the *Scotsman*, *Dunfermline Press* and *Journal*, a description of the building, " Clark's Guide to Dunfermline," and the coins of the realm.

Mrs. Carnegie next spread the mortar over the stone, after which the coping was lowered into its place along with the ornamental finial. The stone was then plumbed and levelled ; and after Mrs. Carnegie had given the three mystic taps, she said, "I declare this memorial stone duly and properly laid, and may God bless the undertaking."

The Provost, addressing Mrs. Carnegie, said : "In the name of the Free Library Committee, I have now to present you with this trowel, with which you have this day done this great work. An inscription has yet to be put upon it, which will show to the people who come after you what you were enabled to do this day." (Cheers.)

Mrs. Carnegie having bowed her acknowledgments, most of the company proceeded to St. Margaret's Hall, to partake of the splendid luncheon there provided, and take part in the other proceedings of the evening.

The large crowds were very orderly all day, and there was very little undue crushing. Superintendent Stuart and the burgh police, assisted by Superintendent Chisholm and a number of the county force, maintained excellent order during the day.

LUNCHEON IN ST. MARGARET'S HALL.

Shortly after six o'clock, after the interesting ceremony of laying the memorial stone, Mrs. and Mr. Carnegie and friends were entertained at a grand luncheon in St. Margaret's Hall, where covers were laid for 260. The hall was gayly decorated with numerous flags, bannerets, and flowering shrubs, and presented a very fine appearance. Above the platform there was suspended a white flag bearing the following inscription printed in blue,

"Welcome to the Noble-Hearted Andrew Carnegie;" while at the other end of the hall, below the gallery, was one with the following words: "To the Strangers a Kind Welcome." In addition to the ladies and gentlemen at the tables, the gallery was filled with ladies, who evinced a warm interest in the proceedings. Provost Walls presided, and ex-Provost Mathieson and Mr. W. Inglis acted as croupiers. On the chairman's right were Mrs. Carnegie, New York; Mrs. D. O. Hill, Edinburgh; Mr. Phipps, Pittsburgh; Miss Franks, Liverpool; Mr. and Mrs. McCargo, Pittsburgh; and Miss A. Lauder, Dunfermline; and on the left the honored guest of the evening; Colonel and Mrs. Myers, Dunfermline; Miss J. Johns, Pittsburgh; Mr. McCandless (Mr. Carnegie's secretary), New York; Mr. Vandevort, Pittsburgh; Miss French, Davenport; Miss Graham, Wolverhampton; and Miss Roxburgh, Edinburgh. The assemblage was a thoroughly representative one, and included many of the working classes. Rev. Dr. Mitchell said grace, and after a sumptuous repast, served up in Mr. Anderson's, of the City Arms Hotel, best style, the Chairman proposed the health of "The Queen," which was duly honored.

The Chairman: "I ask you now to drink to the health of another potentate who, though not a crowned monarch as our most gracious Queen, rules over one of the most powerful empires in the world —the health of Mr. Garfield, the President of the United States. (Cheers.) It is not often we have the privilege of drinking to the health of the President; but seeing that we have so many of his distinguished subjects before us, I am sure you will drink his health as heartily as we have drunk that of our Queen's. The President has come before us lately in a very painful manner, enough to shock the feelings of every one of us. We lately heard of another crowned head being assassinated, which was to be deplored, but not so much to be wondered at, although he was a monarch who had conferred vast benefits on his country ; and because he did not go so far as some wished he was assassinated. Our own beloved Queen has not been free from the terror of the assassin ; but to think that such a man, so noble as President Garfield, who himself has risen to the high position he holds by his own efforts—who was elected to it by the votes of his fellow-citizens—who was respected by all persons, and was equally at home in the Senate as in the Sunday-school—that such a man should be the mark for the assassin to shoot at was a great wonder indeed. I can assure our American friends here that we felt as deeply as they did what had been done to that noble gentleman. I am glad to see that the President is likely to recover ; and I now propose his health, coupled with that of Colonel Myers, the representative of America in Dunfermline." (Cheers.)

Colonel Myers, in reply, said : " The President of the United States has my hearty sympathy, and I am sure he has all yours as well. We all rejoice at the favorable prospects of his speedy recovery from the wounds inflicted by a lunatic. (Cheers.) I say a lunatic, because it is hard for us to believe that any man in his sound senses should attempt to take the life of the President of the United States—(cheers)

—a man in whom the milk of human kindness flows to overflowing, and in whose bosom no place is left for anger, animosity, or hostility to any human being alive. (Cheers.) I have met President Garfield on the battle-field when thousands were lying around slain, but yet although he had the spirit of warfare in him, when you looked on his calm face you could not but feel that it was not possible for him to treat his fallen foes with any act of tyranny or of oppression. (Cheers.) I say, I repeat, we rejoice at the prospect of his speedy recovery, which will be shared by all the civilized word, for the crime of assassination is one which all civilized communities must abhor. It is the act of the coward; it is the act of the insane; it is the act of one that we all shun, and must of necessity shun, because life has no value if the assassin is applauded for his deed. (Cheers.) We are here to-day to do honor to Mr. Carnegie, who is on a visit at the present time to his native place; and although he is a citizen of my country, and you have no longer an exclusive claim on him—although he is rich, and has any amount of the comforts of this life to be able to procure all the luxuries that money can buy, yet by his generous and liberal gifts to this town, he has shown to you and to the world that he has not forgotten the people in the 'Auld Gray Toon.' (Loud cheers.) I was pleased to see you turn out so well as you did to do honor to a poor weaver's son. (Cheers.) I was pleased to see a demonstration which, I am sure, some of your old heads never expected to see, when you saw him leave this town to seek his fortune in the far West. It is to me a great pleasure that I can at this time point out to you Mr. Carnegie as a living example of what industry, energy, honesty, and sobriety can do for a man in the noble and great Republic of the West. (Cheers.) Probably every one of you have relatives or friends out in America, and you are aware that there we look upon the poorest as equal in rights to the richest. We have no nobility there, and every man is noble who behaves himself. Therefore, it gives me great pleasure to point out to you Mr. Carnegie, who has risen by his own efforts to prominence, respect, and plenty. (Cheers.) The demonstration held to-day was one I did not expect to see from the people of Dunfermline, for they are generally so cold, and not easily roused to enthusiasm. I see, however, that when you are put on your mettle, and you are requested to turn out, you have no hesitation in doing so in a style befitting a prince, even although it is only to the son of a weaver." (Cheers.)

"The Prince and Princess of Wales and the other members of the Royal Family" were next proposed by the Chairman, after which followed "The Army, Navy, and Reserve Forces," coupled with the name of

Lieutenant Martin, who, in the course of his reply, stated that he had known Mr. Carnegie from the time they were boys, and he had all along given evidence of attaining the high position which he now held. To the best of his recollection, Mr. Carnegie was at the head of every class he was in at school, and he held a high position among the other boys of the school. He knew that by comparison, for he had felt it to his own disadvantage several times. They

had all seen a boy at the school come out complete
from top to toe with a bit of collar over his coat of
about three inches. Such a boy was Mr. Carnegie
—(cheers)—and what he was then he is now in all
respects. He then gave evidence of a high ambition, and he had no doubt that the success he had
attained was very much due to his having an ambitious and excellent mother. (Cheers.)

Ex-Provost Mathieson next gave " The Health of
Mr. Carnegie." "You have intrusted me with a
toast," he said, "which properly, from its importance, should have come from the chair, and under ordinary circumstances I would have felt it to be an arduous task to propose the toast of the evening. Under the circumstances, however, in which we are
met to-day, I don't see that any speaking on my
part is required, as from the events which have taken
place this day there is enough to show Mr. Carnegie
the respect in which he is held by his native city—
(loud cheers)—and any remarks I might make in proposing his health would only have the effect of weakening any feelings that may have arisen in his bosom
from what has occurred to-day already. (Cheers.)
I think you will all agree with me when I say, that,
so far as Dunfermline is concerned, the turn-out to-day has been one which has not been witnessed before, even by the very oldest inhabitant. (Cheers.)
I think that Mr. Carnegie was right when he said to-day that it was more like an ovation given to an emperor on his return from his conquests than the reception of a private citizen visiting his native town.
(Cheers.) Now, I think that, so far as Mr. Carnegie
is concerned, he richly deserves the ovation he has

received. In all my historical readings— in Scotland at least, and even abroad—I don't think that there is any crowned monarch returning to his country, even after declaring peace, that could have turned out a procession such as we had to-day. (Cheers.) I endeavored to time the procession as it passed, and as nearly as I could make out, it was more than a mile in length, and three-quarters of that mile was composed of ladies. (Laughter and cheers.) From Alexander the Great and Napoleon Bonaparte, there has been no monarch or emperor at a procession such as that we have seen to-day. (Cheers.) I attribute it to the fact that Mr. Carnegie is a bachelor. (Loud laughter.) On a former occasion, at a meeting at which Mr. Carnegie was present, and when I occupied the chair which the Provost now holds, I made the remark that the only flaw in Mr. Carnegie's character was that he wanted a wife. (Laughter and cheers.) I attribute that very much to the fact of his having a mother. (Laughter.) His mother has taken good care over him, and has showed that she does not want to hand him over to the tender mercies of some half-cousin, or any of the half-dozen young ladies who are with him to-day. (Laughter.) I assure you that I was a little observant of Mr. Carnegie when the large procession of ladies was passing, and I noticed that when any one a little better looking than the others passed, he was quite fascinated—(laughter and cheers)—and if some of the American ladies fail to fascinate him, perhaps some of the Scotch will. In the events of to-day there were some incidents of a touching character, but there was one which indicated to me the true nobility of Mr. Carnegie's mind, and that was—not the presenting of the Baths nor the Library to the town—but that, when passing along, he called a halt opposite the very humble dwelling in Moodie Street in which he first saw the light. (Loud cheers.) That showed to me, that although the dwelling was low, his character was high. (Renewed cheers.) Now, I won't detain you any longer, except to say that I hope that the inhabitants of Dunfermline who heard Mr. Carnegie's address in the public park to-day will take the advice he then gave, and make a good use of the means he has given them to improve their minds. The motto he has put over the doorway—'Let there be light'—means that every one who enters the Library is to obtain light in the way of learning; and I hope the working classes of Dunfermline will take full advantage of it. (Cheers.) I have now to ask you to drink to Mr. Carnegie's health. His character has been well expressed in the motto on the flag above the platform—'The Noble-hearted Andrew Carnegie'—and I hope you will now give this toast a hearty reception."

The toast was responded to with much enthusiasm, the ladies in the gallery rising to their feet and waving their handkerchiefs, while the whole company sang lustily, "He's a jolly good fellow."

Mr. Carnegie said, in reply: "Will you kindly permit me first to offer some kind of explanation to my good American friends as to what this ovation means. This procession—those thousands of comely, saucy maidens—(laughter and cheers)—the trades and all classes of Dunfermline vying with each other; and the very complimentary speech which my friend has felt himself justified in making, and, above all, the vociferous cheers with which my mother and I have this day been greeted—(cheers)—for it is not to be supposed that these strangers know that every one who has the good fortune to claim this spot on earth as his birthplace is received when he returns from exile with such warmth and affection, as needs very little excuse to burst forth in such a demonstration as that which we have this day witnessed—(loud cheers)—this reception, I say, is in no sense personal, for neither my mother nor myself would be able to appear here to-day if we were not enabled to see clearly that for the moment we but symbolize the intense love and devotion which every true son and every true daughter of Dunfermline bears to this lovely spot of earth—the ancient metropolis of Scotland—which we all love so well. (Prolonged cheers.) Sir, my first duty is now, on behalf of my good mother, to tender to the members of the Free Library Committee her heartfelt, deep, and earnest thanks for the large share assigned to her in this day's proceedings. (Cheers.) The future historian of Dunfermline, writing her annals, perhaps a thousand years hence—the Dr. Henderson of that period—must, and will, record that on this day, amid the brightest of sunshine and the plaudits of assembled thousands, my mother was privileged to rank her name with the annals of her native town in, perhaps, the most enduring of all forms which it is possible to devise. Believe me when I say that in her estimation and in that of her sons—the one absent as well as the one who now addresses you—no honor which Queen

Victoria has it in her power to bestow could rank
with this. (Loud cheers.) And, gentlemen—I beg
pardon, ladies, for it is most agreeable to me as a
bachelor to find ladies present to honor us at this
banquet—believe me, that deep as is our attachment,
unbounded our admiration, for the great and glorious Republic of the West—(cheers)—that land which
said to my parents, with outstretched arms, ' Come,
be with us, be of us, and share on equal terms with
the most favored of our own children the magnificent heritage with which we are blessed '—(renewed
cheers)—that country which has taken and so grandly nursed us in her generous bosom—(cheers)—saying to us, ' Here there is no kingcraft, no priest-
craft, no law of primogeniture and entail, no
proud hereditary rank above implying your infe-
riority below '—I say, deep and unbounded as
our love for that land is, still, my friends, Scotland is our own, our native land (cheers); and
still is Dunfermline our home and all which that
sacred word implies. (Renewed cheers.) I said to-
day that in America we care not whence a man
springs; our Lincoln was a rail-splitter, and our Garfield a boy on the canal. But permit me now to tell
you that it is a sweet and gracious thing to come to
one's home, where we know our fathers and grand-
fathers lived. And, to-day, when driving up to the
town, one of the most charming of young ladies
stopped us, and kindly handed me a bouquet. On the
little card was written, ' From the College of Patiesmuir.' (Laughter and cheers.) Many of you are old
enough to remember the College of Paticsmuir, and
you have all heard of it. (Laughter.) Well, sir, if I

am proud of anything I am proud of my lineage, and my grandfather was professor at the College of Patiesmuir. (Great laughter.) But I have something else to be proud of on the other side, because you knew my grandfather, Thomas Morrison, and you knew my uncle, Thomas Morrison—(cheers)—and you remember the Bailie. (Renewed cheers.) My friends, I have been very much afraid that Scotland had slipped back in the matter of education; but I am delighted to tell you that in my progress through Scotland, nothing has given me greater satisfaction than to see the new and beautiful schools, with the masters' houses adjoining—showing to the world that Scotland is not disposed to yield even to America supremacy in the important duty of providing education for her children, and that she intends that the weapons which have hitherto been wielded so successfully as to create the unusual stir which three and a half millions of her sons have made throughout the world shall be so wielded in the future, and that her sons shall go forth as well equipped for the battle of life as any— thus making sure that Scotland will continue to contribute her full share to the progress of the world. (Loud cheers.) Nothing has given me greater pleasure than the meeting in Dunfermline, at which all ranks and classes, vying with each other—the pulpit, the press, the learned professions, and that of medicine and the general people—accepted the Free Libraries Act in the most harmonious and enthusiastic manner. Now, this is what I hope will exist in Dunfermline, that whatever differences you may have on political subjects—and all your discussions in Dunfermline are of the very liveliest kind—(laughter)—I hope that when you enter the threshold of this Free Library, you will all shake hands and agree to be brothers. I hope you will cherish and encourage it, and hold it as dear to you as the name and fame of Dunfermline, which we all so much love and admire. (Cheers.) For myself, permit me to say that I have never, during all my life, given funds for any institution of a public nature with feelings of such unalloyed satisfaction as those which prompted me to give them for this Free Library. (Loud cheers.) There is in most enterprises of a charitable nature a suspicion that the good to be produced from them may not be real, but with regard to this Free Library, I know it can work no evil, and I do know it must work lasting good. (Cheers.) In the changes which must come, agencies to which at present we attach great importance may be discarded, and new agencies, of which to-day we know nothing, may arise, which will produce great results; but of this I am convinced that whatever may rise or whatever may fall, the Free Library will stand a never-failing fountain of good to all the inhabitants of Dunfermline. (Prolonged cheers.) Therefore I feel that it is among the blessings for which I have to thank a kind Providence, that the proud privilege has been reserved to me to found a Free Library in my native town." (Loud and prolonged cheers, during which Mr. Carnegie resumed his seat.)

Mr. W. Inglis said: "It falls to my lot to propose a most interesting and important toast. Indeed, I feel convinced, notwithstanding all that has been said, and so well said, by ex-Provost Mathieson, and by the gallant Colonel previous, that my toast is in reality *the* toast of the evening. (Cheers.) I feel sure that for once in my life everybody will agree with me in this. I have now to propose ' The Health of Mrs. Carnegie,' mother of our distinguished guest. (Cheers.) I am sure we are all delighted to see her present on this occasion; and, indeed, my opinion is that this meeting would not have been half so interesting or half so imposing as it is had she not been present. (Cheers.) If she is not the proudest woman and the happiest mother this day in the whole world, I certainly think she ought to be (cheers); for to few mothers falls the pleasant duty which we have seen so gracefully performed by Mrs. Carnegie a little while ago. Not many mothers have such a son to be proud of (cheers), and I may also say that not many sons have such a mother. (Renewed cheers.) Personally, I have very little acquaintance or knowledge of Mrs. Carnegie, but without any one telling me anything about her I venture to say, and I do so with all confidence, that Mr. Carnegie owes much to his mother. It is a fact well known by all, that most men who have risen to eminence, or have attained a high position of any kind, have been greatly indebted to the loving and constant influence of their mother. (Cheers.) This, I have no doubt, has been the case with Mr. Carnegie. Allow me to say, that the influence of a good mother is such that good and worthy sons such as Mr. Carnegie are proud of, and know how to value. (Cheers.) I think our guest did well when he suggested to the members of the Free Library Committee that his mother should lay the memorial stone of the very handsome building which he has so generously gifted to his fellow-townsmen. In doing so, I think he honored himself as well as honored his worthy and respected mother; for in doing so, he manifested a trait of character which we cannot but admire, and which we would all do well to imitate. (Cheers.) The Free Library will always, in my opinion, be associated in the minds of the Dunfermline people with the beautiful affection existing between Mrs. Carnegie and her son. (Cheers.) The Library will prove a great power in refining, elevating, and educating the people, and I am very glad, indeed, to think that the people of Dunfermline have endeavored to show their gratitude to Mr. Carnegie for his handsome gifts. (Cheers.) I ask you now to get to your feet, and drink with all enthusiasm the health of Mrs. Carnegie."

The toast was most enthusiastically responded to.

Mr. Phipps, with whose name it was coupled, said: "Mr. Chairman, Ladies, and Gentlemen, it gives me great pleasure to reply to this toast. I only regret my inability to do so in the manner I should like to do. The subject is here, the occasion is here, and the orator only is lacking. Since my early childhood to the present time it has been my good fortune to be uninterruptedly on the most friendly terms with the good lady whom we to-day delight to honor. Her home to me has been a second home, and she has been to me like a mother, and her sons like brothers; and, therefore, you will appreciate the fact when I state it, that I feel all the diffidence and backwardness that one would feel in speaking of a near and dear relative. It is like praising one's own. (Applause.) When a young child, Mrs. Carnegie taught me how to tell the time of day; in later years, endeavored to teach me the value of time. Like household words I have listened to Mrs. Carnegie telling, in a manner pleasant and suited to a childish ear, the first stories I ever heard of Scottish history—the noble, valorous deeds of 'Scots wha hae wi' Wallace bled,' the tales of Bruce, and others. How deeply they sank into the young minds of those who listened! Whenever I think of patriotism—of love of country—Mrs. Carnegie is to me the representative. With what pleasure the neighbors' children would listen with bright eyes to Mrs. Carnegie reciting from memory portions of the 'Lady of the Lake,' 'Marmion,' and other poems. I can assure you Robbie Burns was not forgotten. 'A man's a man for a' that,' 'John Anderson my Jo, John,' and many other pieces, were familiar to the children of the neighborhood long before they could read them. Mrs. Carnegie's was the home where many friends delighted to visit —her heart was kind to young and old, and her mind entertaining to all. With what pleasure she spoke of her native land! Scotland always seemed to be in her mind, and she never forgot Dunfermline. Is it to be wondered at that, when with her eldest son I first landed in this interesting ancient city, I felt as though I was treading my own native soil? If it was not my land, it was my friend's land—it was my partner's land—and I felt and claimed an interest in it. We will not allow Scotland alone to claim Sir Walter Scott and Robert Burns any more than we will allow England to claim Shakespeare—these gods among men are ours; they are the world's. Noble sentiments, once uttered, are no longer the property of one people or one nation—they are the property of the world. We glory in them and claim them; they are ours—ours to cherish and love. The early stories the kind neighbor and friend had told me came rushing back to memory, and I thanked her in my heart. I speak of self, but to the circle of friends she was always alike kind and good, and to all the neighborhood she was widely known for kindness, for her good judgment, for her liberality in lending or giving from her little store. If assistance of any kind was needed, it was Mrs. Carnegie who was sought for. (Applause.) No lady whom I have known has so wide a circle of friends—rich and poor, high and low—and to all she is alike kind, and by all classes beloved and respected. (Applause.) Mrs. Carnegie has lived for her sons. What but her affection for her family could have induced her to tear herself away from other near kindred and her other dear friends, her native land, the scenes of her childhood? Why, she must have suffered greatly in sundering those dear ties; but, however painful, self was not considered, the New World promised a wider field for her sons. Those who have only travelled on the best steamers of the present day can but little imagine the difficulties, the pains, the dangers, that beset an Atlantic journey in those early days, and, as they must have been, the long, weary weeks of passage, instead of, as now, only days; poor sailor as I am, I would almost as soon have gone down as across. (Laughter.) But this sacrifice was nothing to Mrs. Carnegie—she was not to be deterred by what to many would seem like insurmountable obstacles. Mrs. Carnegie has lived for her sons—her self-denial, her teachings, are worthy of all praise. (Applause.) Many a touching tale could be told of her self-sacrificing labors, how she toiled early and late, and how in many ways she denied herself, that her boys might benefit, and nobly have her sons repaid her. The one here to-day has lived for his mother, and his mother has lived for him. Like the Roman matron, Mrs. Carnegie may well point to her sons and say, 'These are my jewels;' may every mother in the land say the same. (Applause.) The donations which Mr. Carnegie has made, small and large, in the past and in the present, are but the natural growth and outcome of the benevolence and liberality of his loved mother. Aye, to her teachings is he not only indebted for this openhandedness, but he is fully as much indebted to her for his ability to be liberal. 'Tis from his noble mother he inherits the talent to acquire means, as well as the disposition to do good with it. All who know the mother and sons, know how much in mental qualities they resemble each other. (Applause.) On the steamer a little incident occurred; a mock trial was held, the defendant was thought to be in for it, but he wisely called Mrs. Carnegie for his counsel, and, despite the opposition of her son, who used his best argument to procure conviction, against the defender was arrayed the whole table. The claimant and his case were very popular, but, notwithstanding, the good old lady not only cleared the defendant, but cleared him triumphantly, and the universal verdict of that company was that the son owed to his mother his talent in argument, and many a good story could be told how profitable this talent has been made by the son. There is but one lady I know in the world to whom I would more readily go for advice, and none to whom I could with greater advantage apply. This is the way all her friends feel. The ability which has enabled the sons to give employment to thousands—the enterprises which have benefited Pittsburgh and Western Pennsylvania, which have made comfortable the homes of so many, and which have quenched not a few, which have scattered plenty and happiness around—this ability has come from the lady who is the subject of our toast, and from the sainted father, as well as the mother, comes equally the poetic taste, the love of fairness, friendship, liberality, and the love of justice and of right, and which has made the son's word as good as a bond. I cannot help saying, 'God bless all good fathers and mothers.' What a noble object they have in life to live for, and how well they may be repaid! (Applause.) America is a fine climate; here is a lady who has undergone the fatigue of coaching from Brighton to Dunfermline. You can all appreciate how laborious it must have been, but no complaint, no breaking down; fresh and as lively as the youngest, she has continued the journey, and will no doubt continue to the end. Can any lady surpass it in all Dunfermline? At Mrs. Carnegie's advanced age, it would seem evident that transplanting is a good thing, and that a residence of more than a third of a century in that hot and cold country, the United States, does not diminish strength.

Try it; come to America; we want the canny, thrifty Scotch, an' we canna get too muckle o' them. (Laughter.) Uncle Sam is rich enough to give us all a farm. I cannot sufficiently express, for our honored friend, the pleasure, the great gratification, and the joy which this day properly affords her. No object which could, perhaps, be set did so well meet Mrs. Carnegie's views as a Free Library. It will afford to all one of the purest and best of pleasures; few can compare with it, and for instruction none can surpass. If I had consulted Mrs. Carnegie on the subject, I feel sure she would have directed me to say to the young particularly, 'Make a good use of the books, read them carefully, lay to heart and benefit by their good teachings.' Let the books of her acquaintance, and her son's friend, Mr. Samuel Smiles, have a good place on the shelves, and in the popularity of the readers such books as Smiles' 'Industrial Biographies,' 'Self-Help,' 'Thrift,' and others, cannot fail to benefit, to improve, to make stronger in the battle of life, every thoughtful reader. In closing, I would say that if Mrs. Carnegie was addressing you she would no doubt express the hope that the library may be to her native city all the donor could ask for. I thank you on behalf of Mrs. Carnegie for your kindness to her, and beg to assure you that this day is, and ever will be, the brightest of bright days of her long and useful life." (Applause.)

The Rev. Mr. Dunbar: "To me has been intrusted the very honorable duty of commending to your best feelings and hopes 'The Carnegie Free Library.' (Cheers.) I am very glad to believe that that is a matter which will so easily come to the hearts of you all, for it is to me a very light duty to commend it unto you. Brevity is commonly said to be the soul of wit, and I think that this evening when we have so many toasts on the programme, all of first-class importance and interest, the proverb is exceptionally true. But although brevity is thus necessary, I cannot allow this matter to pass without speaking two words. The first of them is this, that I have the greatest pleasure in commending this toast to your cordial reception, because it concerns a library. I don't think that my training in life has been of such a kind as to make me underrate a valuable collection of books, seeing that I have all along been occupied in reading books from almost, you might say, my birth ; and no words which I could use, however warm, can sufficiently express the joy and gratification which I and we all feel to-day in having laid the memorial stone of a building which is to contain a vast treasure open to the appreciation of the inhabitants of this town. (Cheers.) I have no doubt that in this library there will be books representing the literature of many countries ; but even were we to go no farther than our own country, and have only British literature, our library would be a great treasure indeed. The British race is a strong and sturdy race, and our conquests in peace and war are known to the whole world ; but among the noblest of our conquests, I think we may put down our rare English literature. (Cheers.) For one thing, it is written in a language which, if a philologer or philosopher looks at for the first time, is said to be the most difficult and curious in the whole world ; but, notwithstanding its peculiarity, there is a pith and a power in our language which have been making their own way all the world over; and I believe that the day shall come when, by dint of perseverance, our language shall become the universal language of mankind. (Cheers.) In this curious yet powerful language, we have a literature which is surpassed by no language which any man ever spoke or wrote in; and the presentation of this Library to us means that there will be thrown open to the acquisition of all our people—if they care to put themselves to the necessary trouble to enter into it—this magnificent heritage, which has come down to us by the genius and labors of our illustrious ancestors. (Cheers.) I am sure that we will respond heartily to the appeal that Mr. Carnegie has himself made, and that we will treasure the Library and use it with all diligence. Now, for my second word to commend this toast to you. I cannot help commending this toast with all heartiness, on account of Mr. Carnegie. (Cheers.) I have no wish to trespass on other people's property in his remarks, but I cannot forget that this is not a Library merely, but the 'Carnegie Free Library,' which has been given to us by the large-hearted generosity of one of our own citizens. (Cheers.) I think we all feel that not only in the matter of this gift of the Library we have cause to love and admire Mr. Carnegie, but in others as well, and the good qualities and abilities which he possesses. (Cheers.) I speak with some personal knowledge of Mr. Carnegie, for we seem to have the faculty of running up against each other every now and again—at Cairo, for example, Wolverhampton, and other places; and he one day remarked, in regard to this, that surely it must be intended by Providence that he was appointed to be the means of doing me some good. (Laughter and cheers.) I have always had a high respect for Mr. Carnegie, on account of his excellent qualities in head and heart. We are all proud of him, and we receive this Library very heartily, because it comes from him, and we all join in one ardent hope and prayer that it will continue to be of great benefit to the inhabitants of the spot which gave him birth." (Cheers.)

Mr. Ross: "I felt very highly honored when I was asked to propose the toast of 'The Strangers' to this meeting; but I must confess I felt my occupation was gone this afternoon when I saw the reception these honored strangers received from the citizens of Dunfermline as they entered the public park in their triumphal car. When one talks of strangers it is with feelings of sympathy, and we are disposed to remember the story of the ancient Gideonites, who entered another city—not Dunfermline—long ago on donkey carts, with clothes torn, and water very putrid. It was not so with the strangers we saw to-day, and I think you will agree with me that Dunfermline has already responded to the toast of 'The Strangers.' (Cheers.) Those ladies and gentlemen who are accompanying our friend, Mr. Carnegie, on his visit to this town, can no longer be characterized as strangers, but as intimate friends, not only of Mr. Carnegie, but of the whole inhabitants of Dunfermline. (Cheers.) I think these ladies and gentlemen must have felt very much pleased with the reception they received, and I can assure them that they saw to-day what no visitors ever saw before—the whole of the population of Dunfermline turning out to do honor to them. Colonel Myers has said that Dunfermline was a rather cold place, and the Colonel to some extent is perfectly right. It is, however, only partially true, because Dunfermline was a hot place as well, as was evinced to-day by the hearty reception Mr. Carnegie and his friends received. I don't know much about Mr. Carnegie's friends, but they come here with a good guarantee, with a preconceived notion in their favor in the fact that they are with Mr. Carnegie, for we all know that Mr. Carnegie would not bring any but the cream of America. (Cheers.) Perhaps in them we are entertaining angels unawares—(laughter and cheers)—and I can promise the visitors that they will not be able to find a burgh which combines such ancient lineage with such busy life now as Dunfermline. They would be shown, likely to-morrow, the residences and the tombs of the most ancient kings of the country. They will also see our manufactures, which are keeping pace with the wants of the time, and supplying our American brethren with good linen; while we, in our turn, derive many good things from America. I hope that the strangers have been enjoying their journey, and I have no doubt but that they will be able to look back upon their visit to Dunfermline as one of the brightest spots of their pilgrimage. (Cheers.) If I may be allowed, I would like to alter the toast from 'The Strangers' to 'Our Cousins,' coupled with the name of Mr. McCargo." (Cheers.)

Mr. McCargo said: "I am very glad to know that

you don't consider us strangers. I have heard of Dunfermline, it seems to me, from the first time I heard of anything. Mr. Carnegie has been my most intimate friend all my life; and there is nothing that excels Dunfermline in his estimation, and I may say also in mine too. (Laughter and cheers.) I have also imbibed the deepest affection for Dunfermline from his dear mother; and to-day, when I was riding through your streets, it recalled to my memory all the conversations that I have had with Mr. Carnegie in my early youth about Dunfermline. He was so wrapt up in Dunfermline, that on all possible occasions he dwelt on the people of Dunfermline and the beauty of the country, that I thought you certainly must be a kindly people to inspire such a very deep affection in Mr. Carnegie and his dear mother. Now, I must confess I am very much in love with you as well. (Laughter and cheers.) I don't feel that I am a stranger, and I am of Scotch extraction. (Cheers.) It has been a delightful visit for us to come to this country and see the land that we have heard of so often and read so much about. (Cheers.) You can imagine our feelings when the heather, the bluebell, the broom, and the whin bushes were shown to us. These are things we have heard of since our childhood, and we have all been delighted to see them now. We have had a delightful visit here. It has been a constant ovation, but there is nothing that equals our reception to-day. I feel very proud of Mr. Carnegie because I love him, and I think you simply express his character exactly when you speak of him as the noble-hearted Andrew Carnegie. He is full of love for his fellow-men. He has imbibed those ideas from your authors—Burns, Scott, the Ettrick Shepherd, and many others. The company with whom I am are fully delighted with the reception we have received here. We have had a delightful time of it, and shall remember this day all our lives. You have been very kind." (Cheers.)

Mr. Carnegie next proposed "The Town and Trade of Dunfermline," and in doing so said : If the large number of people they had seen that day depended upon the town and trade of Dunfermline, he was sure they could not approach this toast without some serious thought. Now, he was pleased to learn that notwithstanding the depression which had prevailed in all countries with which he was familiar, the trade of Dunfermline had suffered less than any other of which he had knowledge. (Cheers.) He did not except from the statement so rich a land as that of the American Republic, for the depression there for years had much surpassed anything of which, he was happy to say, the town of Dunfermline had any knowledge for perhaps ten or fifteen years. He asked the gentlemen who were responsible for the trade of the town to take a little bit of advice from him. (Cheers.) They all knew that he had the prosperity of Dunfermline deep at heart, and he was going to call one of the chief sinners to reply to the toast. There had been quite enough of extension in recent years of the trade of Dunfermline, and if they would have a steady and profitable trade they must take care and ça' canny. (Laughter.) He did not say that because he was at all apprehensive that the American demand would cease for their products. America, like every other great country in the world, made efforts to supply its own wants in iron, steel, and woollen goods, and in manufactures generally. She would never relax her efforts until she was master of the situation, and supplied all her great people's needs. He was delighted to say that he excepted from that statement the damask trade of Dunfermline—for there had been no effort in America as yet to interfere with their trade here—and when they went home to America he could safely promise that he and his friends would do their utmost to preserve to the bonny lassies they had seen that day the American market for Dunfermline damask. (Loud cheers.)

Councillor Donald, with whose name the toast was coupled, made a long reply. He was glad of the opportunity of replying, for he felt a very deep interest in the town and trade of Dunfermline, and it would be very strange indeed if he felt otherwise. It was certainly very becoming of Mr. Carnegie to propose the toast, because, to a large extent, the trade, and consequently the town, depended upon the United States of America. He supposed that nearly two-thirds of the goods were sent out there. Mr. Carnegie had mentioned that in order to have a steady and profitable trade, we should ca' canny, but in his opinion this was not a time to ca' canny, but to be up and doing—(cheers) more especially as Mr. Carnegie had told them that the people on the other side of the water were likely to do a great deal more by-and-bye in supplying themselves. He was glad to be able to say that as yet the Americans had done very little in the way of linen manufacturing. They had prospered in every other line, but in that they have not made much progress. He was not afraid of the citizens of America, so far as their own trade was concerned. He remembered some twenty-five years ago when he first landed at New York, that in the leading stores of that city, in Philadelphia and in Boston, he saw the damask linen of Dunfermline being largely sold, but he was sorry to say that on this visit he did not find that their goods were so thoroughly taken hold of as in these days long ago. He found instead that the principal articles in the linen department of the trade were not from Dunfermline, but were from German and Irish manufacturers. They had therefore to compete now with the German and Irish manufacturers. This was not the case before the Exhibition of 1851, but from that date the Germans, French, and the Irish were endeavoring to outstrip them, and they must take care that they did not do them out of the trade altogether. (Cheers.) As to the town, he did not think that Mr. Carnegie expected to see such a fine-looking town, and especially so many fine ladies. (Laughter.) Most of these ladies were power-loom workers, and they were the people who must help them to compete with the Germans and Irish in supplying the Americans with good linen. (Cheers.)

Bailie Seath then proposed " The Health of the Architect." Mr. Walker, he said, was a gentleman well known among them now, and his works spoke for themselves. They had only to look at the Corporation Buildings to see what manner of structure he was qualified to rear, and he thought the Carnegie Free Library Committee had done a good thing in selecting Mr. Walker to design the building. The building, which was now being erected, would form an ornament to the town, as well as a noble example of the generosity of Mr. Carnegie ; and every one had now an opportunity of seeing what the building was likely to be. (Applause.)

Ex-Provost Mathieson replied on behalf of Mr. Walker, who had to leave for Edinburgh with the last train.

Mr. W. Inglis, in proposing "The Health of Provost Walls," said there never was a greater demonstration in Dunfermline before, and they had never had a greater occasion to hold one before. (Cheers.) When he saw the very large procession that day, he felt perfectly proud of the people of Dunfermline. (Cheers.) He was always hopeful that they would rise to a sense of the munificence of Mr. Carnegie in a manner that would show that they really appreciated the kindness and the generosity of their distinguished citizen—(cheers)—and to the labors of the Provost was due, in a large degree, the success of the demonstration.

The Provost suitably acknowledged the toast.

Mr. W. Brown, in a neat speech, proposed the health of the "Croupiers," which was acknowledged by ex-Provost Mathieson.

Mr. Carnegie said they would pardon him if he transgressed from the order of the banquet, as he would like to be permitted to propose "The Health of his friend Bailie Walker." (Cheers.) He got the *Press* and *Journal* every week, and he noticed that in their local Parliament there was a man who—a pawky and canny man—often uttered some words of good common sense—this man was Bailie Walker. (Cheers.) He knew them all and read their speeches in the *Press* when, sometimes, perhaps, he ought to be doing something better; and he must say that there was no reading which furnished him with so much pleasure and—amusement (laughter and cheers), as the proceedings of the Municipal Parliament of the ancient Metropolis of Scotland (renewed laughter and cheers), generally known by the name of Dunfermline. He knew that Bailie Walker would say some sensible thing in reply, and he asked them to drink to the health of Bailie Walker. (Cheers.)

Bailie Walker, in returning thanks, said he had been very much delighted that day till within the last five minutes. (Laughter.) If there was any drawback on his part in coming to meetings, it was in the way of making speeches, which he could not do. As Mr. Carnegie, however, spoke about his pawkiness, he supposed that the best way to show his pawkiness was to be as short as possible. He had, therefore, only to return his sincere thanks to the company for so cordially drinking his health. (Laughter and applause.)

During the evening a number of songs were rendered by several gentlemen, and at the conclusion of the toast list, "Auld Lang Syne" was sung by the company, after which the meeting broke up a little after nine o'clock.

CARNEGIE BATHS.

GRAND SWIMMING COMPETITION.

On Thursday evening, a grand swimming competition took place in the baths, under the auspices of the Carnegie Swimming Club. There was a large attendance of spectators, and among those present were—ex-Provost Mathieson, who presided ; Mr. Carnegie (the generous donor of the baths, and who on entering received a hearty reception); Mr. H. Phipps, Jr. (Mr. Carnegie's partner) ; Mr. D. McCargo, Mr. G. F. McCandless, Mr. B. Vandevort, Mr. A. King, all Mr. Carnegie's American friends ; Provost Walls, Bailies Walker and Steedman ; Councillors Donald, Beveridge, Currie, Alston, and Clark ; Messrs. Reid, Brucefield, J. Drummond, G. Lauder, W. Simpson, W. Reid, Jr., J. and G. Mathewson, W. Wilson, G. Birrell, A. Martin, W. Wilson, Glasgow ; J. Hay, etc.

The Chairman opened the proceedings by making a few remarks, in which he expressed his pleasure at seeing such a large turn-out to welcome Mr. Carnegie. Everything connected with the establishment had been the creation of Mr. Carnegie (applause), and even the means for the performance of the proceedings there that night had been provided by that gentleman also. (Renewed applause.) The Committee of the Swimming Club were highly delighted to see Mr. Carnegie among them again in very good health and spirits. (Applause.) Everything seemed to be favoring him in his journey from the south to the north. He did not think that Mr. Carnegie could have got a better day than yesterday, and although this day was wet and disagreeable, he had no doubt it was only preparatory to a good day on the morrow, to enable Mr. Carnegie to resume his journey. They had been getting their weather regulated lately from America, and he had no doubt that Mr. Carnegie had been telegraphing to the clerk of the weather there the names of the places he was going to stop at, so that he might get a dry day whenever he pleased. (Laughter and applause.) He had now, on behalf of the Carnegie Swimming Club, to present Mr. Carnegie with two documents — one of them being the rules of the Carnegie Swimming Club, and the other a life ticket. (Laughter and applause.) He hoped that Mr. Carnegie would long live to see the swimming in the Carnegie Pond. (Applause.)

The programme was then proceeded with. There was a large number of competitors for each event, and the competition proved to be the best ever held under the auspices of the Society. There were thirteen events, and the spectators watched with keen interest the different races. The programme was carried through with much dispatch, and the arrangements made for the competition were all that could be desired. The principal event of the evening was the 100 yards fast-swimming race—the first prize for which was a handsome medal, presented by Mr. Carnegie, and which was won by G. Wilson. The following are the winners:

Boys' four lengths race, heats (open)—1, J. Millen; 2, D. Balingall; 3, D. M'Laren. Four lengths breast stroke race, heats (open)—1, P. Donald; 2, G. Wallace; 3, A. Colville. Long distance diving, adults—1, W. Todd; 2, C. E. Stewart; 3, W. Brown. Two lengths flying handicap race, heats (open)—1, W. Christie; 2, P. Donald; 3, G. Wilson and J. Taylor, equal. Object diving, adults—1, W. Brown, 13; 2, G. Wilson, 11; 3, C. E. Stewart, 9.

Back race two lengths (open)—1, J. Taylor ; 2, P. Donald ; 3, W. Brown. Boys' distance diving (open) —1, A. Cant ; 2, P. Wright ; 3, J. Millen. 100 yards fast-swimming race, adults (confined)—1, G. Wilson ; 2, W. Christie. Boys' hurdle race, two lengths (open)—1, P. Mollison ; 2, A. Stewart ; 3, G. Millen ; 4, D. M'Laren. Boys' two lengths flying handicap race (open)—1, P. Mollison ; 2, T. Balingall ; 3, J. Millen. Clothes race, two lengths (open)—1, P. Donald ; 2, C. E. Stewart ; 3, A. Colville. Blindfold race, six times across the bath (open)—1, D. Brown; 2, G. Wilson ; 3 A. M'Cansh. Amusing tub race— 1, R. Williamson ; 2, D. Brown ; 3, C. E. Stewart.

At the conclusion of the competition, the Chairman asked Mr. Carnegie to say a few words.

Mr. Carnegie then said : " It is my pleasant duty to-night to ask you to return a vote of thanks to Mr. Mathieson for presiding here this evening. (Applause.) No duty could be more pleasant than that, because he is the man who from the first consented to act as President of the Swimming Club. This exhibition we have witnessed not only with pleasure but with real surprise. (Applause.) It is a hard matter at all times to get a gentleman in ex-Provost Mathieson's position to assume the responsibility of the Presidency of a new society ; but I venture to say that you will have much less difficulty in procuring a successor for the Presidency of the Carnegie Swimming Club—if ever it is necessary to obtain a successor—to ex-Provost Mathieson, which I am sure we all hope will not be for many long years to come. (Applause.) Sir, I think I may venture to congratulate you also upon being President of a club which can do such feats as we have just seen the Carnegie Swimming Club perform. (Applause.) In these days, I hear a great deal upon this side of the water of the loss of empire over the land which is impending over Great Britain. In that kind of talk I take no share whatever, because I think that the world is not done with Great Britain, and I am quite sure that Great Britain is not done with the world. (Applause.) I think that the empire which Britain may have over the earth in the future will be of a different character from that it has hitherto possessed; and I firmly believe, at the same time, that it will be an empire of a higher order—not so much of a physical, but more of a mental character than she has ever exerted upon the destinies of mankind. (Applause.) But however we may differ about that, I think there is one element upon which her supremacy is not likely to be questioned, and that is the water. (Applause.) I think that Great Britain will continue to rule the waves (applause) about as long as I should like to prophecy any nation would rule anything; and I think that it is incumbent for that reason that the sons of Great Britain should learn to be at home in the waves which we expect them to continue to rule. However, there is no longer any question about this, that Dunfermline has begun to see the advantage, and she will no doubt soon recognize the duty, of teaching all her sons to feel this confidence at least, that they were not born to be drowned. (Laughter and applause.) Let me tell you what happened the other day. A boat which had been sailing and had furled its sails was upset. In that boat there was an elderly gentleman, his

wife, and his eldest son. They were 100 yards from
footing, and they were, of course, confused by being
thrown into the water—there being a rope round the
neck of the lady, and one of the gentlemen being en-
tangled in the sail. Nevertheless they swam, sup-
porting each other, to land (applause) and they live
to-day, because every one of them had in youth
learned the art, and I don't hesitate to say the duty,
of knowing how to support himself in the water.
(Renewed applause.) Who was that man? It was
your own city's most distinguished son, Sir Noel
Paton. The lady was Lady Paton, and the other
was his son, Victor. (Applause.) I hope this lesson
will be taken to heart by the good people of Dunfermline. There is one suggestion I should make to
the President. It is this, what we have seen to-
night have been the performances of young men.
Now, I have resided in a young country most of my
life, and I am one of those who believe that a young
country can teach some things to old countries. I
find also that young men have sometimes some
things to teach old men, and I have now to suggest
that I should be most happy to provide the prizes
for, say, a Bailies' race. (Laughter and applause.)
We might also allow Provosts and ex Provosts to
enter (laughter), giving them a start of three or four
seconds. (Renewed laughter.) I would beg further to suggest, subject to your approval, that to
every Town Councillor who would say, 'As sure's
death, I never want to be a Bailie,' we should give
a start of seven or eight seconds (loud laughter), and
if there was a Bailie who would say, 'As sure's
death, I never want to be Provost,' I should give

him any start he liked. (Great laughter.) I would like to know whether that suggestion meets the approval of the young men of the Carnegie Swimming Club. (Loud applause.) Then, I think, we may consider the Bailies' race settled ; and in order that they all may have a fair chance I give them warning now, that upon my next return to Dunfermline I expect to see a splendid race of Bailies. (Applause.) I now thank the Carnegie Swimming Club for the copy of their rules, and the ticket they have presented me, and I assure them it is an honor to have these buildings named after myself. As for the President, I am willing to divide the honors with him on most liberal terms, because he does all the work and I get the greater part of the credit. I only want to say, in conclusion, that I am sure that you have shown these gentlemen from America that if they can boast of their vast prairies and broad lands, that some things have been done here to-night that it would puzzle any city in America to equal." (Loud applause.)

The Chairman thanked Mr. Carnegie for the compliment he had paid him ; and which, had he known all, was rather unmerited, for since he had acted as President the Committee had done all the work. He had looked on at the Committee doing the work, and of course expressed great approval. (Laughter.) He hoped that from that night they would have a large additional number of names added to the membership of the Club ; and from the encouragement they had got from Mr. Carnegie all along, he was sure this would be the case by another year. (Applause.) As to the Bailies' race, he was quite ready, if all the Bailies, the Provost, and Town

Councillors went in for swimming, to be one of them. (Loud applause and laughter.)

The Chairman then presented Mr. Carnegie with a book on swimming, written by Mr. Wilson, Glasgow, which Mr. Carnegie suitably acknowledged.

The proceedings then terminated, and the prizes were presented to the successful competitors at the close.

I will not be tempted to say anything further about this unexpected upheaval except this : after we had stopped and saluted the Stars and Stripes, displayed upon the Abbey Tower in graceful compliment to our American friends (no foreign flag ever floated there before, said our friend, Mr. Robinson, keeper of the ruins), we passed through the archway to the Bartizan, and at this moment came the shock of all that day to me. I was standing on the front seat of the coach with Provost Walls when I heard the first toll of the abbey bell. My knees sank from under me, the tears came rushing before I knew it, and I turned round to tell the Provost that I must give in. For a moment I felt as if I were about to faint. Fortunately I saw that there was no crowd before us for a little distance. I had time to regain control, and biting my lips till they actually bled, I murmured to myself, " No matter, keep cool, you must go on ;" but never can there come to my ears on earth nor enter so deep into my soul a sound that shall haunt and subdue me with its sweet, gracious, melting power like that.

By that curfew bell I had been laid in my little couch to sleep the sleep of childish innocence.

Father and mother, sometimes the one, sometimes the other, had told me, as they bent lovingly over me, night after night, what that bell said as it tolled. Many good words has that bell spoken to me through their translations. No wrong thing did I do through the day which that voice from all I knew of heaven and the great Father there did not tell me kindly about ere I sank to sleep, speaking the very words so plainly that I knew that the power that moved it had seen all and was not angry, never angry, never, but so very, *very* sorry. Nor is that bell dumb to me to-day when I hear its voice. It still has its message, and now it sounded to welcome back the exiled mother and son under its precious care again.

The world has not within its power to devise, much less to bestow upon us, such a reward as that which the abbey bell gave when it tolled in our honor. But my brother Tom should have been there also; this was the thought that came. He, too, was beginning to know the wonders of that bell ere we were away to the newer land.

Rousseau wished to die to the strains of sweet music. Could I choose my accompaniment, I could wish to pass into the dim beyond with the tolling of the abbey bell sounding in my ears, telling me of the race that had been run, and calling me as it had called the little white-haired child, for the last time —*to sleep.*

Friday was a cloudy day, but our friends, Messrs. Walls, Mathieson, Walker, Ross, Drummond, cousin Thomas Morrison, Uncle Lauder, and others who spent the early morning with us and saw us off, unanimously predicted that it would clear. They proved true weather prophets, for it did turn out to be a bright day. Passing Colonel Myers's residence, we drove in and gave that representative of the great Republic and his wife three farewell cheers.

Kinross was the lunching-place. Mother was for the first and last time compelled to seek the inside for a few hours after leaving Dunfermline. These farewells from those near and dear to you are among the cruelest ordeals one has to undergo in life. One of the most desirable arrangements held out to us in all that is said of heaven is to my mind that there shall be no parting there. Hell might be invested with a new horror by having them daily.

We had time while at Kinross to walk along Loch Leven and see the ruined castle upon the island, from which Douglas rescued Queen Mary. What a question this of Mary Queen of Scots is in Scotland. To intimate a doubt that she was not purity itself suffices to stir up a warm discussion. Long after a "point of divinity" ceases to be the best bone to snarl over, this Queen Mary question will probably still serve the purpose. What matters it what she was? It is now a case of beauty in distress, and we cannot help sympathizing with a gentle, refined woman (even if her refinement was French veneering), surrounded by rude, coarse men. What is the use of "argie bargicing" about it? Still, I suppose, we must have a bone of some kind, and this is certainly a more sensible one than the "point of divinity," which happily is going somewhat out of fashion.

To-day's talk on the coach was all of the demonstration at Dunfermline, and one after another incident was recalled. Bailie Walker was determined we should learn what real Scotch gooseberries are, and had put on the coach an immense basketful of them. "We never can dispose of so many," was the verdict at Kinross ; at Perth it was modified, and ere Pitlochrie was reached the verdict was reversed and more wished for. Our American friends had never known gooseberries before, friend Bailie, so they said.

Fair Perth was to be our resting-place, but before arriving there the pedestrians of the party had one of their grandest excursions, walking through beautiful Glen Farg. They were overpowered at every turn by its loveliness, and declared that there is nothing like it out of Scotland. The ferns and the wild flowers, in all their dewy freshness after the rains, made us all young again, and the glen echoed our laughter and our songs. The outlet from the glen into the rich Carse of Gowrie gave us another surprise worthy of record. There is nothing, I think, either in Britain or America, that is equal in cultivation to the famous Carse of Gowrie. They will be clever agriculturists who teach the farmers of the Carse how to increase very greatly the harvest of that portion of our good mother earth. Davie began to see how it is that Scotland grows crops that England cannot rival. Perthshire is a very beautiful county, neither Highland nor Lowland, but occupying, as it were, the golden mean between, and possessed of many of the advantages of both.

PERTH, Saturday, July 29.

The view from the hill-top overlooking Perth is superb. "Fair Perth indeed!" we all exclaim. The winding Tay, with one large sail-boat gliding on its waters, the fertile plains beyond, and the bold crag at the base of which the river sweeps down, arrested the attention of our happy pedestrians and kept them long upon the hill. I had never seen Perth before, and it was a surprise to me to find its situation so very fine; but then we are all more and more surprised at what Scotland has to show when thoroughly examined. The finer view from the hill of Kinnoul should be seen, if one would know of what Scotland has to boast.

Before starting to-day we had time to stroll along the Tay for an hour or two. We were especially attracted by a volunteer regiment under drill upon the green, and were gratified to see that the men looked remarkably well under close inspection, as indeed did all the militia and volunteers we saw. The nation cannot be wrong in accounting these forces most valuable auxiliaries in case of need. I have no doubt but in the course of one short campaign they would equal regular troops; at least such was the experience in the American war. The men we saw were certainly superior to regulars as men. It is in a war of defence, when one's own country is to be fought for, that bayonets which can think are wanted. With such a question at issue, these Scotchmen would rout any regular troops in the world who opposed them for pay. As for miserable skirmishes against poor half-armed savages, I hope these men would think enough to despise the bad use they were put to.

The villas we saw upon the opposite bank of the Tay looked very pretty—nice home-like places, with their gardens and boat-houses. We voted fair Perth very fair indeed. After luncheon, which was taken in the hotel at Dunkeld, we left our horses to rest and made an excursion of a few miles to the falls, to the place in the Vale of Athol where Millais made the sketch for his celebrated picture called "O'er the hills and far awa'." It is a grand view, and lighted as it then was by glimpses of sunshine through dark masses of cloud, giving many of the rainbow tints upon the heather, it is sure to remain long with us. For thirty miles stretch the vast possessions of the Duke of Athol; over mountain, strath, and glen he is monarch of all the eye can see—a noble heritage. A recent storm is said to have uprooted seventy thousand of his trees in a single night.

The coachman who drove us to-day interested us by his knowledge of men and things—such a character as could hardly grow except on the heather. He "did not think muckle o' one man owning thirty miles o' land who had done nothing for it." His reply to a question was given with such a pawkie expression that it remains fixed in the memory. "Why do not the people just meet and resolve that they will no longer have kings, princes, dukes or lords, and declare that all men are born equal, as we have done in America?"

"Aye, maan, it would hae to be a *strong* meeting that!"

That strong was so *very* strong; but there will be one strong enough some day, for all that. We cannot stand nonsense forever, patient as we are and slow.

Dunkeld is the gateway of the Highlands, and we enter it, singing as we pass upward.

> "There are hills beyond Pentland
> And streams beyond Forth;
> If there are lords in the south
> There are chiefs in the north."

We are among the real hills at last. Yonder towers Birnam, and here Dunsinane Hill. Mighty master, even here is your shade, and we dwell again in your shadow. The very air breathes of Macbeth, and the murdered Banquo still haunts the glen. How perfectly Shakespeare flings into two words the slow gathering darkness of night in this northern latitude, among the deep green pines:

> "Ere the bat hath flown
> His cloister'd flight; ere, to black Hecate's summons,
> The shard-borne beetle, with his drowsy hums,
> Hath rung night's yawning peal, there shall be done
> A deed of dreadful note. . . . . . .
> . . . . . . *Light thickens;* and the crow
> Makes wing to the rooky wood:
> Good things of day begin to droop and drowse;
> Whiles night's black agents to their prey do rouse."

That man shut his eyes and imagined more than other men could see with their eyes wide open even when among the scenes depicted. The light does "thicken," and the darkness creeps upon us and wraps us in its mantle unawares.

PITLOCHRIE, Sunday, July 30-31.

This is a famous resort in the Highlands; and deservedly so, for excursions can be made in every direction to famous spots. We visited the hydropathic establishment in the evening, and found something resembling an American hotel. Such establishments are numerous in England and Scotland.

Few of the guests take the cold-water treatment, as I had supposed, but visit the hotels more for sake of a change, to make acquaintances, and to "have a good time," as we say. I have no doubt that a month of Pitlochrie air is highly beneficial for almost any one.

We walked to the falls of Tummel, and spent some happy hours there. Cousin Eliza is up in Scotch songs, and I start her every now and then. It has a charm of its own to sit on the banks of the very stream, with Athol near, and listen to the inquiry finely sung:

> "Cam ye by Athol,
> Lad wi' the philibeg,
> Down by the Tummel
> And banks of the Garey?"

Through these very glens the mountaineers came rushing,

> "And with the ocean's mighty swing
> When heaving to the tempest's wing
> They hurled them on the foe."

There is a new meaning to the song when Davie pours it forth in the glen itself:

> "Sweet the lavrock's note and lang,
> Lilting wildly up the glen,
> But aye to me it sings ae sang,
> Will ye no come back again?"

What a chorus we gave him! There are some days in which we live more than twenty-four hours; and these days in Scottish glens count for more than a week of ordinary life. We are in the region of gamekeepers and dogs. It is the last day of July, and the whole country is preparing for the annual massacre of the 12th of August.

The prices paid for a deer forest in Scotland are absurd. Twenty-five to fifty thousand dollars per annum for the right to shoot over a few thousand acres of poorly timbered land, and a force of gamekeepers and other attendants to pay for besides.

For the present the British are what is called a sporting people, and the Highlands are their favorite hunting-grounds. Their ideas of sport are curious. General Sheridan told me that, when abroad, he was invited to try some of their sport, but when he saw the poor animals driven to him, and that all he had to do was to bang away, he returned the gun to the attendant. He really could not do this thing, and the General is not very squeamish either. As for hunting down a poor hare—that needs the deadening influence of custom.

The first of all our glens is the pass of Killiecrankie, through which we walked on our way northward to-day—nothing quite so wild so far. The dark, amber-brown rushing torrent is superb swirling among the rocks, down which it has poured through æons of time, wearing them into strange forms. The very streams are Scotch, with a character all their own, portraying the stern features of the race, torn and twisted by endless ages of struggle with the rocks which impeded their passage, triumphantly clearing their pathway to the sea at last by unceasing, persistent endeavor. The sides of Scotia's glens are a never-failing source of delight, the wild flowers and the ferns seem so much more delicately fine than they are anywhere else. One understands how they affected Burns.

Some of our ladies, mother always for one, will delay the coach any time to range the sides of the glen; and it is with great difficulty that we can get them together to mount once more. The horn sounds again and again, and still they linger; and when they at last emerge from the copse, it is with handfuls or rather armfuls of Nature's smiles—lapfuls of wild flowers—each one rejoicing in her trophies, happy as the day is long, only it is not half long enough. Go the sun down never so late it sinks to its rest too soon.

DALWHINNIE, August 1.

Our drive from Pitlochrie to Dalwhinnie, thirty-two miles, was from beginning to end unsurpassed—mountain and moor, forest and glen. The celebrated falls of Bruar lay in our route, and we spent two hours walking up the glen to see them. Well were we repaid. This is decided to be the finest, most varied fall of all we have seen. The amber torrent works and squirms itself through caldrons there, and gorges here, and dashes over precipices yonder, revealing new beauties and giving us fresh delights at every step. No gentle kiss gives this Scotch fiend to every sedge it overtaketh in its pilgrimage, for in truth, dashing and splashing against the rocks, the surging, boiling water, with its crest of sparkling foam, seems a live spirit escaping from the glen and bounding to the sea, pursued by angry demons behind. Standing on the bridge across the Bruar, one need not be entirely off his balance to sympathize to some extent with the wild wish of my young lady friend, who thought if she had to be anything dead she would be a plunging, mad stream like this, dancing among the rocks, snatching to its breast, as it passed the bluebell and the forget-me-not, the broom and the foxglove, leaping over precipices and tossing its gay head in sparkling rainbow sprays forever and ever.

It was while gazing at this fall that Burns wrote the petition of Bruar water. The shade asked for has been restored—" Clanalpine's pine, in battle brave," now fill the glen, and the falls of the Bruar sing their grateful thanks to the bard who loved them.

I have often reminded you, good readers, that the coaching party, with a few exceptions, hailed with delight every opportunity for a walk. Contrary to expectation, these came much less frequently in Scotland than in England. Far away up among the towering hills, where the roads necessarily follow the streams which have pushed themselves through the narrow defiles, we get miles and miles in the glens along the ever-changing streams ; but it is too level for pedestrianism unless we reduce the pace of the coach and walk the horses. It is after a two hours' climb up the glen to see such a waterfall as the Bruar that we return to the coach feeling, as we mount to our seats, that we have done our duty. We were many miles from our lunching site, and long ere it was reached we were overtaken by the mountain hunger. When we arrived at the house on the moors where entertainment had been promised us, it was to find that it had been rented for the season for a shooting-box by a party of English gentlemen, who were to arrive in a few days. The people, however, were very kind, and gave us the use of the house. Few midday halts gave rise to more gayety than this, but there is one item to be here recorded which is peculiar to this luncheon. For the first and only time the stewardess had to confess that her supplies were exhausted. Due allowance, she thought, had been made for the effects of Highland air, but the climb to Bruar, " or the brunt of the weather," had produced an unusual demand. The very last morsel was eaten, and there seemed a flavor of hesitancy in the assurance some of us gave her that we wished for nothing more. There was not even one bite left for the beautiful collies we saw there. Has the amount and depth of affection which a woman can waste on a collie dog ever been justly fathomed? was a question raised to-day ; but our ladies declined to entertain it at all unless " waste" was changed to " bestow." I accepted the amendment. Many stories were told of these wonderful pets, and what their mistresses had done for them. My story was a true one. Miss Nettie having to go abroad had to leave her collie in some one's care. Many eligible parties had been thoughtfully canvassed, when I suggested that as I had given her the dog it might be perfectly safe to leave him with me, or rather with John and the horses. A grave shake of the head, and then, " I have thought of that, but have given it up. It would never do. Trust requires *a woman's care.*" Not a smile, all as grave as if her pet had been a delicate child. " You are quite right," I replied ; " no doubt he would have a dog's life of it at the stable." She said yes, mournfully, and never suspected a joke. But if the ladies must go wild over some kind of a dog, let it be a collie. I like them myself a little.

It was gloaming ere we reached Lake Ericht, twelve hundred and fifty feet above the sea, and entered the queer little inn at Dalwhinnie. A bright fire was made, and we were as gay as larks at dinner. I am sure nothing could surprise Americans more than the dinners and meals generally which were given us even in such out-of-the-way stations as this. Everything is good, well cooked, and nicely served. It is astonishing what a good, nice dinner and a glass of genuinely old claret does for a party after such a long day's drive and a climb.

Reassembling after dinner in our neat little parlor, the Stars and Stripes displayed as usual over the mantel, we were all as fresh and bright as if we had newly risen, and were in for a frolic. The incidents of the day gave us plenty to talk about—the falls, the glen, that mountain blue, the lake, and oh! that first dazzling glint of purple heather upon the high rock in the glen which drew forth such exclamations! A little patch it was which, having caught more of the sunshine there than that upon the moors, had burst before it into the purple and given to most of us for the first time ample proof of the rich, glorious beauty of that famous plant.

What says Annie's song?

"I can calmly gaze o'er the flowery lea,
I can tentless muse o'er the summer sea;
But a nameless rapture my bosom fills
As I gaze on the face of the heather hills."

Aye, Annie, the "nameless rapture" swells in the bosom of every Scotchman worthy of the name, when he treads the heather.

Andrew Martin's prize song, "The Emigrant's Lament," has the power of a flower to symbolize the things that tug hardest at the heart-strings very strongly drawn. By the way, let it be here recorded, thanks to friend John Reid, This is a Dunfermline song, written by a minister, the Rev. Mr. Gilfillan—if his sermons were equal to this, he should have stood high in the kirk—three cheers for Dunfermline! (that always brings the thunder, aye, and something of the lightning too). The Scotchman who left the land where his forefathers sleep sings:

> "The palm-tree waveth high, and fair the myrtle springs,
> And to the Indian maid the bulbul sweetly sings;
> *But I dinna see the broom* wi' its tassels on the lea,
> Nor hear the linties sang o' my ain countrie."

There it is, neither palm-tree nor myrtle, poinsetta nor Victoria Regina, nor all that luscious nature has to boast in the dazzling lands of the south, all put together, will ever make good to that woe-begone, desolate, charred heart the lack of that wee yellow bush o' broom—never! Nor will all "the drowsy syrups of the East" quiet the ache of that sad breast which carries within it the dooms of exile from the scenes and friends of youth. They cannot agree, in these days, where a man's soul is, much less where it is going; let search be made for it close, very close, to the roots of that ache. It is not far away from that centre which colors the stream of man's life.

Many times to-day, in the exhilaration of the moment, one or another enthusiastic member called out, "What do ye think o' Scotland noo?" and even Emma had to confess in a half-whisper that England was nothing to this. Perry and Joe had never been beyond the borders before, and gave in their adhesion to the verdict—there was no place like Scotland. "Right, Perry!"

We have never seen the paragon of grace, the Scottish bluebell, in its glory till now. It is not to be judged in gardens; it is not in its element there; but steal upon it in the glen and see how it goes to your heart. Truly I think the Scotch are the best lovers of flowers, make the most of them, and draw more from them than any other people do. This is a good sign, and may be adduced as another proof that the race has a tender, weak spot in the heart to relieve the hard level head with which the world credits them.

Whew! Thermometer 53° during the night, the coldest weather experienced during our journey. But how invigorating! Ten years knocked off from the age of every one of us, excepting from that of several of the ladies, who could hardly spare so much and still be as charming.

We were stirring early this morning, in for a walk across the moors, with the glorious hills surrounding us. A grand walk it was too, and the echoes of the horn came all too soon upon us. Looking back down the valley of Lake Ericht, we had the ideal Highland view—mountains everywhere fading into blue in the distance, green to their tops except when capped with snow, and bare, not a tree nor a shrub to break their baldness, and the lake lying peacefully among them at the foot of the vale. These towering masses

> "Seem to stand to sentinel Enchanted Land."

I am at a loss for any scenery elsewhere with which to compare that of the Highlands. The bluish tinge above, the rich purple tint below, the thick and thin marled, cloudy sky with its small rifts of clear blue, through which alone the sun glints to relieve the dark shadows by narrow dazzling lights— these give this scenery a weird and solemn grandeur unknown elsewhere; at least I have seen nothing like it. During my strolls at night amid such scenes, I have always felt nearer to the awful mysteries than ever before. The glowering bare masses of mountain, the deep still lake sleeping among them, the sough of the wind through the glen, not one trace of man to be seen, no wonder it makes one eerie, and you feel as if

> "Nature had made a pause,
> An awful pause, prophetic of its end."

Memory must have much to do with this eerie feeling upon such occasions, I take it, for every scrap of Scottish poetry and song bearing upon the Highlands comes rushing back to me. There are whispering sounds in the glen:

> "Shades of the dead, have I not heard your voices
> Rise on the night-rolling breath of the gale?
> Surely the soul of the hero rejoices
> And rides on the wind o'er his own Highland vale."

I hear the lament of Ossian in the sough of the passing wind.

We stopped at the inn at Kingussie, one of the centres of sporting interest, but drove on beyond to spread our luncheon upon the banks of the Spey, close to the ruins of Ruthven Castle, a fine ruin in this beautiful valley of the Spey. We walked to it after luncheon. It was here that the Highland clans assembled after the defeat of Flodden Field and resolved to disband, and the country was rid of the Stuarts forever. How far the world has travelled since those days! The best king or family of kings in the world is not worth one drop of an honest man's blood. If the House of Commons should decide to-day that the Prince of Wales is not a fit and proper figure-head, and should vote that my Lord Tom Noddy is, there is not a sane man in the realm who would move a finger for the rightful heir; yet our forefathers thought it a religious duty to plunge their country into civil war to restore the Stuarts—

"A coward race, to honor lost;
Who knew them best despised them most."

But I suppose they were about a fair average of royal races. It does one good to mark such progress. I will not believe that man goes round in a circle as the earth does; upon the king absurdity he has travelled a straight line. When we made kings by act of Parliament (as the Guelphs were made), another lesson was learned, that Parliament can unmake them too. That is one bloody circle we need never travel again. Not one drop of blood for all the royal families in Christendom. Carried, *nem. con.*

We even hear of a second step proposed: no more marriage portions for extravagant, riotous princes to set disgraceful examples with, and three Cabinet Ministers saying Amen. I rather enjoy the spectacle of the royal family begging hat in hand. It is such a splendid lesson, such a grand thing for us to be proud of coming from "the fountain of honor." (Don't laugh, that is what they call it.) Bah! let them earn an honest living like the rest of us. That will be the upshot of all this, one of these happy days; for the present, let us congratulate ourselves that the great-grandson of the man who would have died for Prince Charlie grumbles at even *paying* for Prince Leopold.

Boat o' Garden was to be our refuge, a small, lovely inn on the moors, the landlady of which had telegraphed us in a rather equivocal way in response to our request for shelter. There was no other house for many miles, so we pushed on, trusting to our star. We were all right. The house was to be filled on the morrow with sportsmen, and we could be entertained "for this night only." Such is luck. Even as it was, the family rooms had to be given up to us; but then, dear souls, there is nothing they would not do for the Americans. As for the coach, there was no building on the moors high enough to take in the huge vehicle; but as showing the extreme care taken of property in this country, I note that heavy tarpaulins were obtained, and it was nicely covered for the night. What a monster it seemed standing out in the darkness!

After dinner we received packages of the Dunfermline papers containing the full account of the demonstration there and of the speeches. It goes without saying that there was great anxiety to read

the account of that extraordinary ovation. Those
who had made speeches and said they were not very
sure what, were seen to retire to quiet corners and
bury themselves in their copies. Ah, gentlemen, it
is of no use! Read your orations twenty times
over, you are just as far as ever from being able to
gauge your wonderful performances; besides the
speech made is nothing compared to any of half a
dozen you have since made to yourself on the same
subject. Ah! the Dunfermline people should have
heard these. So sorry! One can tell all about the
speeches of his colleagues, however, and we made
each other happy by very liberal laudations, while
we each felt once more the generous rounds of applause with which we had been greeted.

After mailing copies of the newspapers to numerous friends, there came a serious cloud over all. This
was to be our last night on the moors; the end of
our wayward life had come. One more merry start
at the horn's call, and to-morrow's setting sun would
see the end of our happy dream. Arcadia would be
no more; the Charioteers' occupation would be gone.
It was resolved that something should be done to
celebrate the night to distinguish it from others.
We would conform to the manners and customs of
the country and drink to our noble selves in whiskey
toddy with Highland honors. This proved a success. Songs were sung; Aaleck was in his most
admirable fooling; "your health and song" went
round, and we parted in tolerably good spirits.

There was an unusual tenderness in the grasp of
the hand, and mayhap something of a tremor in the
kind "Good-night, happy dreams," with which it

was the custom of the members to separate for the night, and we went to bed wondering what we had done to deserve so much happiness.

—·

BOAT O' GARDEN, August 2.

Inverness at last! But most of us were up and away in advance of the coach, for who would miss the caller air and the joy of the moors these blessed mornings when it seems joy enough simply to breathe? But did not we catch it this morning! No use trying to march against this blow; the wind fairly beat us, and we were all glad to take refuge in the school-house till the coach came; and glad were we that we had done so. Was it not a sight to see the throng of sturdy boys and girls gathered together from who knows where! for miles and miles there are seen but a few low huts upon the moors; but as some one has said, "Education is a passion" in Scotland, and much of the admitted success of the race has its root in this truth. The poorest crofter in Scotland will see that his child gets to school.

Note this in the fine old song,

"When Aaleck, Jock, and Jeanettie
Are up and got their lair,
They'll serve to gar the boatie row
And lichten a' our care."

Heavy is the load of care that the Scotch father and mother take upon themselves and struggle with all the years of their prime that the bairns "may get their lair." To the credit of the bairns let it be noted that the hope expressed in the verse just quoted

is not often disappointed. They do grow up to be
a comfort to their parents in old age when worn
out with sacrifices made for them. Our great men
come from the cradles of poverty. I think he was a
very wise man who found out that the advantage of
poverty was a great prize which a rich man could
never give his son. But we should not condemn the
Marquises of Huntley, the Dukes of Hamilton, and
the rest of them; they never had a fair chance to
become useful men. It is the system that is at
fault, and for that we the people are responsible. The privileged classes might turn out quite
respectably if they had justice done them and
were permitted to start in life as other men are.
For my part, I wonder that they generally turn
out as well as they do. The kite mounts only
against the wind. People of rank might cease to
occupy the present dull level their class presents and
mount too if we did not " come between the wind
and their nobility." Do be just. We sow for me-
diocrities, and we get them. Why should not the
aristocracy furnish a Darwin or a Huxley, a Watt
or a Bessemer, a Robertson Smith, a Gladstone or a
Disraeli, a Princeps or a Millais, a Mill or a Spencer,
a Carlyle or a Macaulay, or a *somebody*, just once?
No reason in the world. It has not escaped doing
so by miracle, but only by being spoiled by pamper-
ing. What a statesman Edmund Burke was! the
greatest England has yet produced. None of his
speeches show his grasp more clearly than that in
which he said: " Kings are naturally lovers of low
company. It must indeed be admitted that many
of the nobility are as perfectly willing to act the part

of parasites, pimps, and buffoons, as any of the lowest of mankind can possibly be."

If Edmund Burke said that, why may I not quote it here? But does it not amaze you that the gentlemen of England—and they are the gentlemen of the world—remain responsible in these days for such a system? Education, early education, alone accounts for it. They do not think, but they have much to answer for here. I move that justice be done, and prince and duke be placed upon terms of equality with the best of us. We should not handicap any of our fellow-citizens so fearfully.

While revelling in the exquisite beauty of England, such quiet and peaceful beauty as we had never seen before, the thought often came to me that I should be compelled to assume the apologetic strain for my beloved Scotland. It could not possibly have such attractions to show as the more genial South, but so far from this being so, as I have already said, there was scarcely a morning or afternoon during which the triumphant inquiry was not made, " What do you think of Scotland noo?" Of all that earned for Scotland the first place in our hearts I note the pretty stone school-houses, with teacher's residence and garden attached, which were seen in almost every village, and if I had no other foundation than this upon which to predict the continued intellectual ascendency of Scotland and an uninterrupted growth of its people in every department of human achievement, I should unhesitatingly rest it upon these school-houses. A people which passes through the parish school in its youth cannot lose its grasp, or fall far behind in the race. Indeed, compared with the thorough education of the people, the lives and quarrels of politicians are petty in the extreme. It is with education as with righteousness, seek it first and all political blessings must be added unto you. It is the only sure foundation upon which to rear the superstructure of a great state, and how happy I am to boast that Scotland is not going to yield the palm in this most important of all work. No, not even to the Republic. From what I saw of the new schools, I'll back their scholars against any lot of American children to-day ; but I admit one great lack : the former would strike you as somewhat too deferential, disposed to bow too much to their superiors in station, while American boys are said to be born repeating the Declaration of Independence. No more valuable lesson can be taught a lad than this : that he is born the equal of the prince, and what privileges the prince has are unjustly denied him. It would do Scotch boys good to hear my young American nephews upon the doctrine that one man " is as good as another and a good deal better." Of the sights which cause me to lose temper, one is to see a splendid young Briton, a real manly fellow, standing mum like a duffer when he is asked why the son of the Guelph family or of any other family should have a privilege denied to him. Are you less a man ? Have not you had as honest parents and a better grandfather ? Why do you stand this injustice ? And then he has nothing to say. Well, I have sometimes thought I have noticed the cheek a little redder. That is always a consolation. Thank God ! we have nothing like this in America. Our young men carry in their knapsacks a President's seal, and no one is born to any rank or position above them. Under the starry flag there are equal rights for all. It will be so in Scotland perhaps ere I die (D. V.).

I do not think I have spoken of the announcements of amusements seen everywhere during the trip throughout the rural districts : band competitions, cricket matches, flower shows, wrestling matches, concerts, theatricals, holiday excursions, races, games, rowing matches, football contests, and sports of all kinds. We are surprised at their number, which gives uncontestable evidence of the fact that the British people work far less and play far more than their American cousins do. No toilers, rich or poor, like the Americans! The band competitions are unknown here, but no doubt we shall soon follow so good an example and try them. The bands of a district meet and compete for prizes, which stirs up wholesome rivalry and leads to excellence. I do not know any feature of British life which would strike an American more forcibly than these contests. We should try one here, and, by and by, why not an international contest?—the Dunfermline band playing the "Star-Spangled Banner" and the Pittsburgh performers "Rule Britannia:" yes, that's right ; I insist upon "Rule Britannia"—that is the nation's song ; I'm growing tired of "God save the Queen"—even such a model as the present one is only personal, after all. I wish Her Majesty well, but I love my country more. "Rule Britannia" is the national song ; the other is only personal.

I hope Americans will find some day more time for play, like their wiser brethren upon the other side.

We came to the crossing of the Spey to-day to find that the long high bridge was undergoing extensive repairs and closed to travel. In America it would never have occurred to us that a bridge should be closed while being rebuilt, but in the science of bridge-building British engineers are a generation behind us. However, there was nothing for it but to follow down the stream until another bridge was found. When we did find it, we saw a notice prohibiting loads beyond two tons from crossing. It was a light iron structure (perhaps a Tay blunder upon a small scale). The wind was whistling like a fiend about our ears as it came roaring down the glen ; all pleasant while we were in the woods skirting the river with our backs to it, but when we turned to cross it seemed as if we should be blown bodily from the top of the coach. Everything was taken off the top, and we all dismounted. Perry and Joe drove over, while we all walked, some of us on the lea side of the coach for shelter, and in a few minutes we were so sheltered in the glen again as scarcely to know there was a breath of air stirring ; but these " Highland homes where tempests blow" know what gales are. We have had great blows now and then at some high points crossing the moors, for the hills you rarely cross ; these you have to avoid, but to-day was the only time we were compelled to dismount.

We had not far to drive before we reached the pretty little burn which falls into the Findhorn, the spot selected for the last luncheon.

But here was the burn, the burnie of Ballantyne, and I repeated, as I now do from memory, that gem. Listen to the story of the burnie. No, you shall only have one verse of it to tempt you to read it all for yourselves:

> "And ither burnies joined and its rippling song was o'er,
> For the burn became a river ere it reached the ocean shore,
> And the wild waves rose to greet it with their ain eerie croon,
> Working their appointed work and never, never done."

Isn't that pretty? This spot seemed made to order: the burn, the fire, the mossy grass, the wild river, the moor and glen, all here. Down sat the Charioteers for the last happy luncheon together. We were all so dangerously near the brink of sad regret that a bold effort was necessary to steer clear of thoughts which pressed upon us. We had to laugh for fear we might cry, the smile ever lies so near the tear. It *had* to be a lively luncheon, that was all there was about it. Aaleck and Ben and Davie and Gardie all knew this, and when duty calls it doesn't take much to start our boys to frolic. A few empty bags which we had used for horsefeed in emergencies suggested a sack-race. Such roars of laughter when one or the other of the too ambitious contestants went to grass! This was a capital diversion. Any one looking down upon us (but in these lonely glens no eye is there to see) would never have imagined that this sport was started only as a means to prevent the travellers becoming mournful enough for a funeral. A little management is a great thing: it pulled us through the last luncheon with only tears of laughter.

"In, Joe! Right, Perry! Sound the horn! All aboard for Inverness!" There was something in the thought, "We have done it," which kept us from regret, although the rebuke came sharply from the ladies, as one pointed out another milestone, "Oh, don't, please!" With every white stone passed there was a mile less of Arcadia to enjoy. Over moor and dale lies the way, a beautiful drive, gradually descending for many miles, for we have from twelve hundred and fifty feet above sea level at Dalwhinnie to a few hundred only near Inverness.

At last the call is made, "Stop, Perry!" Capital of the Highlands, all hail! Three rousing cheers for bonnie Inverness! There she lies so prettily upon the Moray Firth, surrounded by fields of emerald green, an unusually grand situation and a remarkably beautiful town. We stopped long upon the hill-top to enjoy the picture spread out below. The Charioteers will forget much ere their entrance into Inverness fades from the memory. A telegram from our ex-general manager, friend Graham, conveyed to us the congratulations of our Wolverhampton connection upon the triumphant success of our expedition, to which something like this was sent: "Thanks! We arrived at the end of this earthly paradise at six o'clock this evening. When shall we look upon its like again?"

INVERNESS, August 3.

It was Saturday, 6 P.M., August 3d, exactly seven weeks and a day after leaving Brighton, when we entered Inverness and sat down in our parlor at the Caledonian Hotel. Up went the flags as usual; dinner was ordered; then came mutual congratulations upon the success of the journey just finished. Not one of the thirty-two persons who had at various times travelled with us ever missed a meal, or had been indisposed from fatigue or exposure. Even Ben had been improved by the journey. Nor had the coach ever to wait five minutes for any one ; we had breakfasted, lunched, and dined together, and not one had ever inconvenienced the company by failing to be in time.

How shall I render the unanimous verdict of the company upon the life we had led ?

"I never was so happy in my life. No, Aaleck, not even upon my wedding journey." That is the verdict of one devoted young wife, given in presence of her husband.

"I haven't been so happy since my father took me fishing, and I wasn't as happy then," was Aaleck's statement.

"Oh, Andrew, I have been a young girl again!" We all know who said that, Miss Velvety.

"I can't help it, but I don't want to speak of it just now. It's too sad." Prima donna, this was a slightly perilous line to follow, for the heart was evidently near the mouth there.

"To think of it, Naig, I have to go home tomorrow." That was Eliza.

"Jerusalem the golden ! it would make a wooden Indian jump, this life would." No need of putting a name to that, Bennie, my lad ; that's Rugby, Tennessee.

"Andrew, I've just been in a dream of happiness all the time." That was the bold McCargo (oor Davie).

"I never expect to be as happy for seven weeks again," met with a chorus of supporters.

Mother, however, put us all in a more gleeful mood by her verdict: "Well, I expect to have another coaching trip yet. You'll see! He can't help doing more of this, and I'll be there. He can't keep *me* at home!" And her hearty laugh and a clap of her hands above her head brought us all merrily to dinner. She's a caution, that young mother of mine; but she is very often a true prophet. We shall see, we shall see!

After dinner we strolled about the city and admired its many beauties, especially the pretty Ness, which flows through the town to the sea. Its banks and islands constitute one of the finest of pleasure-grounds for the people, and many a lover's tale, I trow, has been told in the shady walks beside it. I felt quite sentimental myself sauntering along between the gloaming and the mirk with one of the young ladies. The long, long gloaming of the north adds immensely to the charms of such a journey as this we have just taken. These are the sweetly precious hours of the day.

On reassembling in our parlor an ominous lack of hilarity prevailed. We did manage, however, to get the choir up to the point of giving this appropriate song with a slight variation:

> "Happy we've been a' thegither,
> Happy we've been in ane and a',
> Blyther folks ne'er coached thegither,
> Sad are we to gang awa'."
>
> (Chorus.)

It wasn't much of a success. We were not in tune, nor in time either. Joe and Perry were to come at ten to say good-by. Here the serious business of life pressed upon us, escape being impossible. We had to meet it at last. They came and received the thanks and adieux of all. I handed them notes certifying to all coming coaching parties that fortunate indeed would be their lot were Perry and Joe to take them in charge. Joey responded in a speech which so riveted our attention during delivery that not one of us could recall a sentence when he ceased. This is one of the sincere regrets of the travellers, for assuredly a copy of that great effort would have given the record inestimable value. It was a gem. I have tried to catch it, but only one sentence comes to me: "And has for the 'osses, sir, they are better than when we started, sir; then they 'ad flabby flesh, sir; now they're neat an' 'ardy." So are we all of us, Joey, just like the 'osses; "neat an' ardy," fit for walk, run, or climb, and bang-up to everything.

We had all next day to enjoy Inverness. What a fine climate it has as compared with the Highlands south of it! Vegetation is luxuriant here and the land fertile. One would naturally expect all to be bleak and bare so far north, but that Gulf Stream which America sends over to save the precious tight little isle from being a region of ice makes the region delightful in summer and not extremely cold even in winter. We are assured that the climate of Inverness is more genial than that of Edinburgh, which is not saying very much for the capital of the north surely, but still it is something.

CALEDONIA HOTEL,
INVERNESS, August 5, evening.

General manager at dinner.

To waiter: " What time do we start in the morning ? "

Waiter : " The *omnibus* starts at seven, sir."

Shakespearian Student—" Ah ! There was the weight which pulled us down. The omnibus ! Farewell the neighing steeds, the spirit-stirring horn, whose sweet throat awaked the echoes o'er mountain and glen. Farewell, the Republican banner, and all the pride, pomp, and circumstance of glorious coaching, farewell ! The Charioteers' occupation's gone."

First Miltonic Reciter—

> " From morn till noon,
> From noon till dewy eve,
> A summer's day we fell."

Our fall from our own four-in-hand to a public omnibus—oh, what a fall was there, my countrymen !—involved the loss of many a long summer's day to us—long as they had been the sun ever set too soon.

It was all up after this. Perry and Joe, the coach and the horses were speeding away by rail to their homes ; we were no longer *the* coaching party, but only ordinary tourists buying our tickets like other people instead of travelling as it were in style upon annual passes. But fate was merciful to us even in this extremity ; we were kept from the very lowest stage of human misery by finding ourselves alone and all together in the omnibus ; our party just filled it. If it was only a hotel omnibus, as one of the young ladies said, it was all our own yet, as was the MacLean boat at the flood, and the ladies, dear souls, managed to draw some consolation from that.

We returned from Inverness by the usual tourist route: canal and boat to Oban, where we rested over night, thence next day to Glasgow. Under any other circumstances I think this part of the journey would have been delightful. The scene indelibly impressed upon our minds is that we saw at night near Ballahulish. I remember a party of us agreed that what we then saw could never be forgotten. But Black alone could paint it. It is saying much for any combination of the elements when not one nor two, but more of a party like ours stand and whisper at rare intervals of the sublime and awful grandeur which fascinates them into silence; never am I lifted up apparently so close to the Infinite as when amid such weird, uncanny scenes as these. We had an hour of this that night, fitting close to our life in the Highlands of Scotland.

The first separation came at Greenock. Mother, Emma, and Mr. and Mrs. King disembarked there for Paisley. The others continued by boat to Glasgow and enjoyed the sail up the Clyde very much. It was Saturday, a holiday for the workers. The miles of shipyards were still, "no sound of hammers clanking rivets up," that fine sunny day, but as we passed close to them we saw the iron frames of the future monsters of the deep, the Servia, Alaska, and others destined to bear the palm for a short time, and then to give place to others still greater, till the voyage between England and America will only be a five-day pleasure excursion, and there will be "two nations, but one people." God speed the day! But the old land must come up to Republicanism! I make a personal matter of that, Lafayette, my boy, as Mulberry Sellers says. "No monarchy need apply." We draw the line at this. All men were created free and *equal*. Brother Jonathan takes very little "stock" in a people who do not carry out that fundamental principle.

We landed at the Broomielaw, whither father and mother and Tom and I sailed thirty odd years ago, on the 800-ton ship Wiscasset, and began our seven weeks' voyage to the land of promise, poor emigrants in quest of fortune; but, mark you, not without thoughts in the radical breasts of our parents that it was advisable to leave a land which tolerated class distinctions for the *one* government of the people, by the people, and for the people, which welcomed them to its fold and insured for their sons as far as laws can give it equality with the highest and a fair and free field for the exercise of their powers.

My father saw through not only the sham but the injustice of rank, from king to knight, and loved America because she knows no difference in her sons. He was a Republican, aye, every inch, and his sons glory in that and follow where he led.

I remember well that Aunty Morrison, Uncle Lauder, Dod, and other friends, stood on the quay and waved farewell. Had their adieu been translated it would have read:

> "Now may the fair goddess Fortune
> Fall deep in love with thee,
> Prosperity be thy page."

Thanks to the generous Republic which stood with open arms to receive us, as she stands to-day to welcome the poor of the world to share with her own sons upon equal terms the glorious heritage with which she is endowed—thanks to it, prosperity has indeed been our page.

At St. Enoch's Station Hotel, Glasgow, the final disbanding of the party took place. A delegation of five members, Mr. and Mrs. McCargo, Misses Johns and French, and Mr. Vandevort, were sent to investigate the Irish question and report at Queenstown. Miss Eliza Lauder returned to Dunfermline. Mother and Miss Franks and Mr. and Mrs. King were visiting the Lambertons at Paisley. Harry and I ran down to see friend Richards at his basic process at Eston, stopping over night at York and Durham, however, to enjoy once more the famous cathedrals and hear the exquisite music.

LIVERPOOL, August 13.

We sailed to-day in the Algeria, the great Servia having been delayed. Many were there to see us off, including four or five Charioteers. The English are, as Davie said, "a kindly people," a warm-hearted, affectionate race, and as true as steel. When you once have them you have them forever. There was far more than the usual amount of tears and kisses among the ladies. One would have thought our American and English women were not cousins, but sisters. The men were, as befitting their colder natures, much less demonstrative. There seems never to be a final good-by on shipboard; at every ringing of the bell another tender embrace and another solemn promise to write soon are given. But at last all our friends are upon the tug, the huge vessel moves, one rope after another is cast off, handkerchiefs wave, kisses are thrown, write soons exchanged, and the tug is off in one direction and we in another. Some one broke the momentary silence and brought the last round of cheers with the talismanic call: "Right, Perry!" That touched all hearts with remembrance of the happy, happy days, the happiest of our lives. So parted the two branches of the Gay Charioteers.

At Queenstown we received the Irish contingent, who had enjoyed their week in the Emerald Isle. Very nice indeed was the report, but with this quite unnecessary addenda, "But, of course, nothing to coaching." That goes without saying in our ranks.

The Algeria was a great ship in her day; now she is sold to a freight line. But when she does not give a good account of herself in a hurricane do not pin your faith in any iron ship. You may still, however, believe that one of steel like the Servia will stand anything. She has at least three times the strength of any iron steamer afloat. When she does not outride the tempest, you may give up in earnest and decide, like Mrs. Partington at sea, never to trust yourself so far out of the reach of Providence again.

On Wednesday morning, August 24th, the party reached New York again, and were finally disbanded. Two or three of the most miserable hours I ever spent were those at the St. Nicholas Hotel, where mother, Ben, and I lunched alone before starting for Cresson. Even Ben had to take an earlier train for Pittsburgh, and I said to mother: "All our family gone! I feel so lonely, so deserted: not one remains." But mother was up to the emergency. "Oh, you don't count me then! You have still one that sticks to you." Oh, yes, indeed, sure of that, old lady.

> "The good book tells of one
> Who sticks closer than a brother;
> But who will dare to say there's one
> Sticks closer than a mother!"

(Original poetry for the occasion.)

These horrid partings again; but whatever the future has in store for those who made the excursion recorded here, I think I can safely say that they could not wish their dearest friend a happier life than that led from June 1st to August 24th by the Gay Charioteers.

Those who have mounted the coach become, as it were, by virtue of that act members of an inner circle; a band of union knits them closely together. To a hundred dear, kind friends in the Beautiful Land we send thanks and greeting. Their kindness to us can never be forgotten, for they soon taught us to feel that it was not a foreign land which we had visited after all, but the dear old home of our fathers.

Forever and ever may the parent land and the child land grow fonder and fonder of each other, and their people mingle more and more till they become as one and the same. All good educated Americans love England, for they know that she alone among the nations has

> "On with toil of heart and knees and hand
> Through the long gorge to the far light hath won
> Her path upward and prevailed."

She it was who pointed out to America what to plant, and how, and where. The people of England should love America, for she has taught them in return that all the equal rights of man they are laboring for at home are bearing goodly fruit in the freer atmosphere of the West. May the two peoples therefore grow in love for each other, and with this fond wish, and many a sad farewell, the Gay Charioteers disband forever afterward in life to rally round each other in case of need at the mystic call of " Skid, Joe," " Right, Perry ;" and certain of this, that whatever else fades from the memory, the recollection of our coaching trip from Brighton to Inverness remains a sacred possession forever.

THE RECORD.

BRIGHTON TO INVERNESS, JUNE 17 TO AUGUST 3, 1881.

		MILES.
June 17.........	BRIGHTON (The Grand Hotel).	
" "	GUILFORD (The White Lion)..................	42
" 18 and 19.	WINDSOR (The Castle)........................	32
" 20.........	READING (The Queen's)	27
" 21.........	OXFORD (The Clarendon).....................	34
" 22.........	BANBURY (The White Lion)...................	23
" 23.........	STRATFORD-ON-AVON (The Red Horse).........	18
" 24.........	COVENTRY (The Queen's).....................	22
" 25 to 30....	WOLVERHAMPTON (English Homes, best of all)...	33
July 1	LICHFIELD (The Swan).......................	20
" 2 and 3 ...	DOVEDALE (The Izaak Walton)................	26
" 4	CHATSWORTH (The Edensor)..................	24
" 5	BUXTON (The Palace)........................	26
" 6	MANCHESTER (The Queen's)..................	23
" 7	CHORLEY (Anderton Hall)....................	14
" 8	PRESTON (The Victoria)......................	16
" 9 and 10...	LANCASTER (The County)	29
" 11.........	KENDAL (King's Arms).......................	22
" 12.........	GRASSMERE (Prince of Wales)................	18
" 13	KESWICK (The Keswick).....................	12
" 14.........	PENRITH (The Crown).......................	16
" 15.........	CARLISLE (The County and Station)...........	16
" 16 and 17..	DUMFRIES (The Commercial).................	32
" 18	SANQUHAR (The Queensberry)...............	28
" 19.........	OLD CUMNOCK (Dumfries Arms)..............	29
" 20........	DOUGLASS (Douglass Arms)..................	28
" 21 to 26....	EDINBURGH (The Royal).....................	44
" 27 and 28..	DUNFERMLINE (The City Arms)...............	16
" 29.	PERTH (The Royal George)..................	32
" 30 and 31..	PITLOCHRIE (Fisher's Hotel)	33
August 1........	DALWHINNIE (The Loch Ericht)...............	32
" 2........	BOAT OF GARTEN (The Boat o' Garten)........	35
" 3........	INVERNESS (The Caledonian).................	29
	TOTAL MILES,	831

www.ingramcontent.com/pod-product-compliance
Lightning Source LLC
Chambersburg PA
CBHW032123230426
43672CB00009B/1837